FISH, FISHING AND FISHERIES

RECREATIONAL FISHERIES IN THE U.S.: SELECTED REPORTS ON POLICY, ECONOMICS AND DATA COLLECTION

FISH, FISHING AND FISHERIES

Additional books in this series can be found on Nova's website under the Series tab.

Additional e-books in this series can be found on Nova's website under the e-book tab.

FISH, FISHING AND FISHERIES

RECREATIONAL FISHERIES IN THE U.S.: SELECTED REPORTS ON POLICY, ECONOMICS AND DATA COLLECTION

ELLEN K. PARKER
EDITOR

New York

Copyright © 2016 by Nova Science Publishers, Inc.

All rights reserved. No part of this book may be reproduced, stored in a retrieval system or transmitted in any form or by any means: electronic, electrostatic, magnetic, tape, mechanical photocopying, recording or otherwise without the written permission of the Publisher.

We have partnered with Copyright Clearance Center to make it easy for you to obtain permissions to reuse content from this publication. Simply navigate to this publication's page on Nova's website and locate the "Get Permission" button below the title description. This button is linked directly to the title's permission page on copyright.com. Alternatively, you can visit copyright.com and search by title, ISBN, or ISSN.

For further questions about using the service on copyright.com, please contact:
Copyright Clearance Center
Phone: +1-(978) 750-8400   Fax: +1-(978) 750-4470   E-mail: info@copyright.com.

NOTICE TO THE READER

The Publisher has taken reasonable care in the preparation of this book, but makes no expressed or implied warranty of any kind and assumes no responsibility for any errors or omissions. No liability is assumed for incidental or consequential damages in connection with or arising out of information contained in this book. The Publisher shall not be liable for any special, consequential, or exemplary damages resulting, in whole or in part, from the readers' use of, or reliance upon, this material. Any parts of this book based on government reports are so indicated and copyright is claimed for those parts to the extent applicable to compilations of such works.

Independent verification should be sought for any data, advice or recommendations contained in this book. In addition, no responsibility is assumed by the publisher for any injury and/or damage to persons or property arising from any methods, products, instructions, ideas or otherwise contained in this publication.

This publication is designed to provide accurate and authoritative information with regard to the subject matter covered herein. It is sold with the clear understanding that the Publisher is not engaged in rendering legal or any other professional services. If legal or any other expert assistance is required, the services of a competent person should be sought. FROM A DECLARATION OF PARTICIPANTS JOINTLY ADOPTED BY A COMMITTEE OF THE AMERICAN BAR ASSOCIATION AND A COMMITTEE OF PUBLISHERS.

Additional color graphics may be available in the e-book version of this book.

Library of Congress Cataloging-in-Publication Data

ISBN: 978-1-63485-595-2

Published by Nova Science Publishers, Inc. † New York

CONTENTS

Preface		vii
Chapter 1	National Saltwater Recreational Fisheries Policy 2015 *National Marine Fisheries Service*	1
Chapter 2	National Saltwater Recreational Fisheries Implementation Plan 2015-2018 *National Marine Fisheries Service*	9
Chapter 3	Recreational Fisheries Year in Review 2012 *National Marine Fisheries Service*	23
Chapter 4	The Economics of the Recreational for-hire Fishing Industry in the Northeast United States 2nd Edition *Scott Steinback and Ayeisha Brinson*	63
Chapter 5	Recreational Fisheries Management: The National Marine Fisheries Service Should Develop a Comprehensive Strategy to Guide Its Data Collection Efforts *United States Government Accountability Office*	119
Index		155

PREFACE

Recreational fishing is a traditional American pastime integral to social, cultural, and economic life in coastal communities across the nation. This time-honored activity allows millions access to America's great outdoors each year, while generating billions of dollars in economic activity. Traditionally shaped by commercial forces, demographic, market, and ecological shifts are changing the nature of U.S. fisheries. Our nation's expansive coastal and ocean resources face increasing pressure as coastal populations grow, and more people pursue recreational opportunities in ecologically important marine and estuarine areas. The purpose of this book is to provide guidance for Agency consideration in its deliberations pertaining to development and maintenance of enduring and sustainable high quality saltwater recreational fisheries. This policy identifies goals and guiding principles to be integrated into NOAA's National Marine Fisheries Service's (NMFS) planning, budgeting, decision-making, and activities, and includes examples of implementation concepts and strategies supported by NMFS. Moreover, this book provides a detailed overview of the operating structure of the "average" Northeast for-hire head boat and charter boat, and estimates the economic activity that for-hire businesses contribute to the Northeast's economy as measured by total employment, labor income, and sales. Lastly, this book examines challenges that have been identified with the NMFS' data collection efforts for managing marine recreational fisheries and steps the agency has taken to improve data collection and challenges that remain.

In: Recreational Fisheries in the U.S.   ISBN: 978-1-63485-595-2
Editor: Ellen K. Parker   © 2016 Nova Science Publishers, Inc.

Chapter 1

NATIONAL SALTWATER RECREATIONAL FISHERIES POLICY 2015[*]

National Marine Fisheries Service

INTRODUCTION

Saltwater recreational fishing is a traditional American pastime integral to social, cultural, and economic life in coastal communities across the nation. This time-honored activity allows millions access to America's great outdoors each year, while generating billions of dollars in economic activity.

Traditionally shaped by commercial forces, demographic, market, and ecological shifts are changing the nature of U.S. fisheries. Our nation's expansive coastal and ocean resources face increasing pressure as coastal populations grow, and more people pursue recreational opportunities in ecologically important marine and estuarine areas.

Beginning with its roots as the Commission of Fish and Fisheries in 1871, NOAA's National Marine Fisheries Service (NMFS) has played a continuous leadership role in science-based stewardship of our nation's living marine resources. NMFS is responsible for maintaining healthy marine and coastal ecosystems capable of supporting sustainable and productive fishery resources for the longterm use and benefit of the nation.

---

[*] This is an edited, reformatted and augmented version of a publication issued by the National Oceanic and Atmospheric Administration, February 2015.

In so doing, NMFS recognizes the substantial benefits to the nation associated with saltwater recreational fishing and is committed to pursuing a collaborative stewardship approach promoting safe public access to fishery resources, fishery sustainability, and regulatory accountability suited to the unique nature of recreational fisheries. To this point, NMFS recognizes the inherent differences between recreational and commercial fisheries and the need for stewardship approaches able to best accommodate each while achieving fishery conservation and management goals.

In February 2014, the non-governmental Morris-Deal Commission published a report highlighting a series of concepts to improve stewardship of saltwater recreational fisheries, including formulation of a national policy. In April 2014, NMFS and the Atlantic States Marine Fisheries Commission conducted the second National Saltwater Recreational Fisheries Summit with constituents from across the nation. NMFS announced its intent to transparently develop a recreational fisheries policy statement for release early in 2015 at the conclusion of the summit.

POLICY PURPOSE, GOALS AND SCOPE

The purpose of this policy is to provide guidance for Agency consideration in its deliberations pertaining to development and maintenance of enduring and sustainable high quality saltwater recreational fisheries. This policy identifies goals and guiding principles to be integrated into NMFS' planning, budgeting, decision-making, and activities, and includes examples of implementation concepts and strategies supported by NMFS.

Consistent with, and in furtherance of, the purposes of the Magnuson-Stevens Fishery Conservation and Management Act (MSA) and other applicable federal statutes, the goals of this policy are to: 1) support and maintain sustainable saltwater recreational fisheries resources, including healthy marine and estuarine habitats; 2) promote saltwater recreational fishing for the social, cultural, and economic benefit of the nation; and, 3) enable enduring participation in, and enjoyment of, saltwater recreational fisheries through science-based conservation and management.

This policy pertains to non-commercial activities of fishermen who fish for sport or pleasure, as set out in the MSA definition of recreational fishing, whether retaining (e.g., consuming, sharing) or releasing their catches, as well as the businesses and industries (e.g., the for-hire fleets, bait and tackle businesses, tournaments) which support them.

This policy recognizes the authorities and responsibilities of other federal natural resource management agencies, regional fishery management councils, interstate marine fisheries commissions, states, tribes, and advisory bodies.

POLICY STATEMENT AND GUIDING PRINCIPLES

It is the policy of NMFS to foster, support, and enhance a broadly accessible and diverse array of sustainable saltwater recreational fisheries for the benefit and enjoyment of the nation. The following six principles will guide NMFS decision-making and activities in the execution of its stewardship responsibilities.

1. Support Ecosystem Conservation and Enhancement

NMFS recognizes a wide range of approaches to restore, maintain, and build diverse healthy marine ecosystems that are foundational to high quality recreational fisheries. Examples of strategies that NMFS supports include:

- Restoration and conservation of habitats that benefit recreational and other fish stocks
- Development and application of best practices to support anglers as stewards of a sustainable environment
- Science-based habitat enhancement activities, including artificial reefs and natural habitats in accordance with Agency policy, which contribute to the conservation and management of recreational fisheries
- Conservation of abundant and resilient forage fish stocks integral to healthy ecosystems and recreational fisheries
- Development and application of aquaculture tools and technologies that support recreational fisheries consistent with existing agency policy (e.g., stock restoration, production of baitfish, shellfish seed for habitat restoration)

2. Promote Public Access to Quality Recreational Fishing Opportunities

NMFS recognizes the fundamental importance of broad public access to healthy and sustainable fisheries resources to recreational fishing. Examples of strategies that NMFS supports include:

- Decision-making that fully considers social, cultural, economic, and ecological factors
- Recurring evaluation of fishery allocations to facilitate equitable distribution of fishing opportunities as fisheries develop and evolve
- Expanding fishing opportunities (e.g., longer-fishing seasons, increased allowable catch levels), when appropriate, based on demonstrated conservation gains
- Understanding and addressing factors affecting angler participation and satisfaction

3. Coordinate with State and Federal Management Entities

NMFS recognizes that improving fisheries science and management is best achieved through collaboration and partnership with state and federal management entities. Examples of strategies that NMFS supports include:

- Aligning program goals and implementation strategies in support of sustainable recreational fisheries
- Enhancing regulatory compliance by improving public awareness and understanding of recreational regulations and through effective enforcement
- Reducing redundancy, leveraging resources, and exploring opportunities for co-management of recreational stocks
- Supporting equitable representation of recreational fisheries interests in decision-making forums

4. Advance Innovative Solutions to Evolving Science, Management, and Environmental Challenges

NMFS recognizes its responsibility to lead and facilitate development of innovative approaches and solutions to evolving stewardship challenges in rapidly changing fisheries environments. Examples of strategies that NMFS supports include:

- Developing and supporting cutting-edge scientific tools and approaches to increase knowledge of recreational fisheries and the marine ecosystems (e.g., acoustic and hi-resolution video surveys, next generation stock assessments)
- Exploring management approaches that have the potential to better accommodate the unique nature of recreational fisheries while achieving conservation mandates
- Encouraging and incentivizing development and use of new gear technology that provides conservation gains (e.g., improves release survival)

Applying creative approaches to problem solving and embracing expertise outside of the Agency (e.g., crowdsourcing, on-the-water experience, external partnerships)

5. Provide Scientifically Sound and Trusted Social, Cultural, Economic, and Ecological Information

NMFS recognizes its pivotal role in providing world class science to facilitate informed decision-making and effective stewardship. Examples of strategies that NMFS supports include:

- Partnering with the fishing, academic, non-governmental, and management communities to develop and implement cooperative research activities on recreational fisheries and integrating defensible results into management
- Collecting recreational catch and effort, social, and economic data that support transparent and participatory management and conservation of saltwater recreational fisheries

- Considering recreational fisheries needs in the prioritization of Agency science activities

6. Communicate and Engage with the Recreational Fishing Public

NMFS recognizes the need to build public confidence and expand understanding of science and management processes. Examples of strategies that NMFS supports include:

- Communicating, in plain language, the basis for and implications of regulatory actions, and the details and results of relevant scientific programs and research
- Listening, understanding, and responding to recreational angler issues and perspectives
- Empowering recreational anglers with information to become resource stewards and effectively engage in the fishery management process

IMPLEMENTATION

The NMFS National Policy for Saltwater Recreational Fisheries is effective upon release and supersedes previous agency policy guidance for saltwater recreational fisheries. This policy will, henceforth, guide NMFS' approach to saltwater recreational fisheries until such time as it is amended or rescinded by the NOAA Assistant Administrator for Fisheries.

The policy will be implemented through consideration and integration of policy goals and supporting principles at all levels within the Agency including office and program level planning, budgeting, and decision-making. NMFS Regional Administrators, Center Directors, and headquarters Office Directors will play a critical role in successful policy implementation, as Agency representatives to the regional fishery management councils and interstate marine fisheries commissions, principal liaisons to state and other federal agencies, and managers of personnel who interact with the public on a daily basis. In addition, the Agency will develop and update national and regional saltwater recreational fisheries implementation plans.

In implementing this policy, it is incumbent upon NMFS to execute its stewardship responsibilities in a manner that minimizes disruptions to, and burdens on, the regulated community while improving public understanding of, and participation in, the regulatory process.

AUTHORITIES AND RESPONSIBILITIES

NMFS' headquarters directorate and office directors, regional leadership (Regional Administrators and Science Directors), and the National Policy Advisor for Recreational Fisheries are responsible for Agency-wide implementation of this policy.

This policy is not intended to, and does not, create any right or benefit, substantive or procedural, enforceable at law or in equity by any party against the United States, its departments, agencies, or entities, its officers, employees or agents or any other person.

In: Recreational Fisheries in the U.S.
Editor: Ellen K. Parker

ISBN: 978-1-63485-595-2
© 2016 Nova Science Publishers, Inc.

Chapter 2

NATIONAL SALTWATER RECREATIONAL FISHERIES IMPLEMENTATION PLAN 2015-2018[*]

National Marine Fisheries Service

A NOTE FROM THE ASSISTANT ADMINISTRATOR FOR FISHERIES

Saltwater recreational fishing is an enormously popular American pastime, economic force, and contributor to conservation. Millions access America's great outdoors through recreational fishing each year, strengthening families, friendships, and communities while contributing billions to the national economy.

NOAA Fisheries believes that saltwater recreational fisheries hold great promise for introducing and connecting the next generation to the natural world while simultaneously presenting complex stewardship challenges, including balancing ecosystem conservation with social and economic benefits for the nation.

Since 2010, the Agency has made substantial progress in developing an internal culture supporting recreational fisheries that recognizes and values recreational fisheries and fishermen. Substantial commitments of staff, time,

---

[*] This is an edited, reformatted and augmented version of a publication issued by the National Oceanic and Atmospheric Administration, April 2015.

and budget have led to regular productive dialogue at the national and regional levels and facilitated action on important issues such as barotrauma and data collection. Most recently, in February 2015, we established a formal National Saltwater Recreational Fisheries Policy, which sets forth goals and guiding principles for our activities to ensure that saltwater recreational fisheries issues are fully considered in our deliberations.

This implementation plan is NOAA Fisheries' first step under the policy, making recreational fisheries a key focus of Agency action. The implementation plan will serve as a basic roadmap for Agency action on recreational fisheries at the national level through 2018. It should be considered a living document, able to accommodate new challenges and opportunities as they arise.

The implementation plan is not an endpoint for our work with the recreational community; it is an additional waypoint on the continuing journey to improve stewardship. NOAA Fisheries will take another important step in 2016 with the release of our regional recreational implementation plans. Finally, the Agency is committed to expanding our capacity to engage the recreational community, including adding new full-time regional recreational fisheries coordinators to help execute the policy while providing an informed representative where people live, work, and fish.

Through this implementation plan and other work, we look forward to continuing constructive dialogue and collaboration with the recreational fishing community to foster, support, and enhance a broadly accessible and diverse array of sustainable saltwater recreational fisheries.

Sincerely,
Eileen Sobeck
Assistant Administrator for Fisheries

INTRODUCTION

NOAA Fisheries is responsible for maintaining healthy marine and coastal ecosystems capable of supporting sustainable and productive fishery resources for the long-term use and benefit of the nation. In February 2015, NOAA Fisheries released the National Saltwater Recreational Fisheries Policy which recognized the importance of saltwater recreational fishing to the nation. Development and issuance of the policy was an important and substantive step toward better understanding the needs of the recreational fishing community and positioning the Agency to address the priorities of recreational anglers across the nation.

The policy identifies goals and guiding principles with respect to the commitment to foster, support, and enhance a broadly accessible and diverse array of sustainable saltwater recreational fisheries. The goals of the policy include:

- Support and maintain sustainable saltwater recreational fisheries resources, including healthy marine and estuarine habitats.
- Promote saltwater recreational fishing for the social, cultural, and economic benefit of the nation.
- Enable enduring participation in, and enjoyment of, saltwater recreational fisheries through science-based conservation and management.

To fulfill this commitment, the Agency will integrate the policy's goals and guiding principles into our activities and deliberations, as with all Agency-wide policies. Recognizing that the value of the policy will come through effective implementation, we see the necessity and benefits of a focused Implementation Plan. This implementation plan describes work NOAA Fisheries will perform in the period 2015 through 2018.

Implementation Plan Structure and Content

NOAA Fisheries will implement the National Saltwater Recreational Fisheries Policy through focused actions using its six guiding principles as an organizational framework. The policy goals are supported by the guiding principles, and the specific actions identified in this plan support and link to one or more of the principles. In short, this document focuses on tangible actions to advance the six guiding principles. This format facilitates tracking and evaluating implementation progress. Successfully implementing the actions identified in this plan will move the Agency incrementally and strategically closer to the policy's overall vision and goals.

The six guiding principles are:

1. Support ecosystem conservation and enhancement.
2. Promote public access to quality recreational fishing opportunities.
3. Coordinate with state and federal management entities.

4. Advance innovative solutions to evolving science, management, and environmental challenges.
5. Provide scientifically sound and trusted social, cultural, economic, and ecological information.
6. Communicate and engage with the recreational fishing public.

Guided by input from fishermen, the general public, management partners, NOAA Fisheries' staff, participants in the National Saltwater Recreational Fisheries Summit (2014), and the policy development process, this document identifies Agency commitments over the next 4 years. It includes currently identifiable Agency commitments for action, primarily from national-level programs, which are within existing budgetary constraints and stewardship mandates. Many of the specific actions support more than one of the six guiding principles, and each of the guiding principles in turn supports more than one of the policy goals.

The Agency will provide biennial reports on implementation status beginning in 2017, allowing for improved accountability and an opportunity to update the implementation plan as appropriate. NOAA Fisheries' work to implement the policy will be expanded in 2016 through the development of region-specific recreational implementation plans using this national framework.

SUPPORT ECOSYSTEM CONSERVATION AND ENHANCEMENT

America's coastal and ocean waters provide an astounding abundance of sustainable living marine resources, which support the most well developed and diverse recreational fisheries in the world. Healthy ecosystems are foundational to the sustainability of these resources and the fisheries that depend upon them. Marine and coastal ecosystems are under pressure from an array of factors such as habitat degradation and loss, invasive species, overfishing, pollution, ocean acidification, and energy development, among others. Building and maintaining high-quality recreational fisheries requires a thoughtful and effective science-based conservation, management, and enhancement approach. Actions supporting this guiding principle include:

Focus on watershed-scale habitat activities that leverage partnerships and directly benefit important recreational fisheries and the communities that depend on them.

- Increase angler engagement in the National Fish Habitat Partnership and NOAA's regional Habitat Focus Areas to better reflect recreational fishing priorities.
- Support angler habitat conservation efforts by increasing awareness of potential federal funding and partnership opportunities.
- Host a workshop to assess the current state of the science, best practices, and potential impacts of artificial reefs.

Take an ecosystem approach to ensuring sustainable fisheries.

- Support research to improve knowledge of ecosystem linkages between inshore habitats and offshore production of recreationally important fishes.
- Advance adoption of release survival techniques and best practices to reduce impacts of recreational fisheries on marine ecosystems by communicating research findings to fishery managers and fishermen.
- Conserve forage fish through targeted habitat restoration projects and by working with partners to provide passage for diadromous forage fish at hydropower dams.
- Conduct surveys at fishing piers to collect data regarding the incidental catch of non-target species, including sea turtles.

Empower anglers as resource stewards.

- Develop angler-friendly guidelines facilitating non-lethal deterrence of marine mammals and safe methods for de-hooking sea turtles and other protected species to reduce angler impacts to NOAA Fisheries' trust resources.
- Enhance public education efforts and partnerships with states and other federal entities (e.g., NOAA's Office of National Marine Sanctuaries) to increase angler awareness of invasive species threats and support angler-based control efforts (e.g., taking lionfish).

PROMOTE PUBLIC ACCESS TO QUALITY RECREATIONAL FISHING OPPORTUNITIES

Access to quality fishing opportunities is a prerequisite to recreational fishing. Working with management partners, fishing access is collectively determined through the Regional Fishery Management Council process. Promoting and supporting access can take many forms, from establishing healthy and abundant stocks of recreationally important fish, to improving the quota allocation process, to accounting for conservation gains when developing regulatory measures. In addition to supporting access to fishing opportunities through participation in the Council process, the Agency will take additional actions to support fishing access. Actions supporting this guiding principle include:
Balance conservation, public access, and economic and social benefits.

- Engage Regional Fishery Management Councils to review harvest allocations on a regular basis to ensure fishery management is achieving goals set forth in the Magnuson-Stevens Fishery Conservation and Management Act (MSA), including issuing guidance developed in partnership with the Council Coordination Committee.
- Present information on conservation gains (e.g., improved post-release survival) to Councils, fostering consideration of expanded recreational fishing opportunities, when appropriate.
- Engage the recreational fishing community in habitat restoration projects (e.g., reef restoration) in NOAA Habitat Focus Areas and other areas to preserve and enhance fishing opportunities and improve ecosystem health.
- Evaluate whether revisions are needed to current regulations under National Standard 10 of the MSA to promote safe recreational access to fisheries.
- Promote the legitimacy and recognition of the economic importance of recreational fisheries within international fisheries management bodies, and seek to maintain and, where feasible and appropriate, expand U.S. recreational fishing opportunities on internationally managed fish stocks.

Promote awareness of quality fishing opportunities through new information and tools.

- Identify and evaluate fishery-focused additions to NOAA electronic nautical charts to assist anglers in accessing fishery resources.
- Collaborate with NOAA's Office of National Marine Sanctuaries to identify and highlight recreational fishing opportunities in national marine sanctuaries.
- Support conservation education and local fishing opportunities for children and non-traditional fishery participants.

COORDINATE WITH STATE AND FEDERAL MANAGEMENT ENTITIES

The complexity of natural resource stewardship requires effective coordination both with the public and also between involved management entities. Strengthening partnerships with federal and state natural resource entities can provide insight and opportunities for effective and alternative approaches to many issues. Sharing scientific, communications, management and enforcement expertise along with aligning management priorities and goals can better leverage resources, eliminate waste, and improve recreational fishing overall. Actions supporting this guiding principle include:

Improve delivery of services to fishermen through strengthened state–federal collaboration.

- Evaluate annually Regional Fishery Management Council balance and communicate findings to state governors to advance equitable stakeholder representation.
- Conduct annual discussions with states to identify shared goals and collaborative opportunities benefiting recreational fisheries.
- Undertake joint state-federal recreational angler education projects to improve understanding of fishery regulations and the importance of compliance.
- Incorporate recreational fisheries issues as a priority in state-federal Joint Enforcement Agreements.
- Engage state and federal agencies through Habitat Focus Areas, Fish Habitat Partnerships, and Landscape Conservation Cooperatives to

identify shared habitat objectives and execution strategies (e.g., ESA section 6 agreements) benefiting recreationally important species.

Bolster connections and collaboration with federal partners.

- Establish regular high-level and staff-level dialogue between NOAA Fisheries and the U.S. Fish and Wildlife Service to strengthen working relationships, explore partnership opportunities, and identify mutual priorities.
- Develop a strategy to expand collaboration between NOAA Fisheries and Sea Grant.
- Work with National Sea Grant Office to incorporate a recreational fisheries focus area into the National Sea Grant Strategic Plans.
- Enhance coordination with the Office of National Marine Sanctuaries, including in identification of potential Sanctuary Advisory Council nominees and focused outreach to recreational fishing interests, to increase angler participation in the Sanctuary management process.
- Develop materials addressing important fisheries science and management issues for recreational fisheries to support improved understanding by Regional Fishery Management Council members.

ADVANCE INNOVATIVE SOLUTIONS TO EVOLVING SCIENCE, MANAGEMENT, AND ENVIRONMENTAL CHALLENGES

NOAA develops and applies cutting-edge techniques to address some of the most pressing environmental issues facing the world today. NOAA Fisheries recognizes our responsibility to lead, support, and serve as a catalyst for private sector innovation to solve the challenging issues of today and tomorrow. Innovation can occur in any area. The range of actions identified below should not be considered constraining; rather it includes areas of interest to the recreational community that are ripe for innovation and action. Actions supporting this guiding principle include:

Support research and technology to benefit recreational fisheries.

- Support scientifically rigorous projects to investigate bycatch and release mortality reduction tools and handling techniques, including through cooperative research and federal grant programs.
- Develop Marine Recreational Information Program certified methods for electronic trip reporting with validation sampling in for-hire fisheries through pilot projects.
- Work in cooperation with the Atlantic Coastal Cooperative Statistics Program and the Gulf Fisheries Information Network to develop the necessary operational and funding plans for implementing for-hire electronic trip reporting programs in the sub-regions where partners desire to implement them.
- Prepare a white paper assessing existing marine, freshwater, and terrestrial natural resource self-reporting applications to understand current uses, limitations, and potential applications in fisheries science and management.
- Pursue electronic reporting through implementation of regionally based NOAA Fisheries electronic monitoring and reporting plans.

Lead scientific efforts to better understand recreational fisheries.

- Develop and implement a Bio-economic Length Structured Angler Simulation Tool (BLAST model) to assess the effects of management actions on angler participation in West Coast recreational fisheries.
- Complete the Main Hawaiian Islands component of National Angler Attitudes and Perspectives Survey, and analyze and distribute the findings to the public and management partners.
- Refine and expand the use of cutting-edge acoustic and hi-definition video survey methods to improve data collection from untrawlable habitat (e.g., reefs) and support fish stock assessments.
- Conduct acoustic tagging and telemetry studies to better understand site fidelity, habitat use, migration, and other behaviors of fish species commonly targeted by recreational anglers (e.g., pilot project at Gray's Reef National Marine Sanctuary, using volunteer recreational anglers to catch, tag, and release target species).
- Execute an economic study of Atlantic highly migratory species fishing tournaments to improve the understanding of their economic impacts and for consideration in management.

- Produce an action plan for discard and release mortality science to guide NOAA Fisheries science efforts related to mortality estimates, improve estimates of mortality, and better incorporate improved mortality estimates into stock assessments.

Pursue management approaches that may better support recreational fisheries.

- Investigate alternative management approaches to recreational fisheries management and satisfaction, specifically including methods based on fishing mortality rates.
- Issue revised guidelines for National Standard 1, addressing management flexibility and fishery stability and including guidelines for implementation of annual catch limits, ecosystem component stocks, and other issues.

PROVIDE SCIENTIFICALLY SOUND AND TRUSTED SOCIAL, CULTURAL, ECONOMIC, AND ECOLOGICAL INFORMATION

The basis of effective natural resource management is sound scientific information. NOAA and its management partners have developed some of the world's most comprehensive and sophisticated recreational fisheries data collection and analysis systems. However, good science is not enough; for the public to have confidence in management there must be confidence in the underlying science. NOAA Fisheries will continue improving the science that underpins management decisions, while working to improve public understanding and confidence. Actions supporting this guiding principle include:

Provide recreational catch and effort information supporting stock assessments and informing management.

- Initiate a National Research Council review of the Marine Recreational Information Program to evaluate current recreational fisheries catch and effort data and science.
- Execute directed projects to improve recreational catch and effort data for pulse and other rare event fisheries, specifically including Gulf of

Mexico red snapper and Atlantic highly migratory species (Large Pelagic Survey).
- Transition to the use of new mail-based recreational fishing effort surveys on the Atlantic and Gulf coasts, including incorporation of new data into stock assessments.
- Identify key areas for habitat mapping to foster improved characterization and assessment of recreational fish habitats.
- Conduct research to evaluate the benefits of natural habitat conservation projects to the health of the ecosystem and their importance to recreationally important fish species.

Bolster understanding of the social and economic importance of recreational fishing.

- Incorporate recreational fisheries as a science priority in Agency and regional science center strategic plans.
- Develop a national strategic plan to guide socio-economic research on recreational fisheries.
- Annually evaluate the status and progress of recreational fishing expenditure, impact, and valuation data collections and assessments for each region through the Recreational Fishing Economic Assessment Index (RFEAI), an internal performance metric.
- Execute a fishing trip expenditure survey in all coastal states to refine understanding of socioeconomic impacts of saltwater recreational fishing.

Empower others to collect, share, and use data.

- Convene recreational fishing groups, states, NGOs, and others to explore potential additional uses of information provided by NOAA observing platforms (e.g., Chesapeake Bay Interpretive Buoy System Update), which may benefit anglers and provide other benefits.
- Engage recreational fishermen in data collection to benefit protected resources recovery and conservation, including: establishing citizen science programs to apply tags and/or report tagged protected species, DNA swabs for stock ID, and photo ID of marine mammals and sea turtles.

- Work with the Office of National Marine Sanctuaries to consider recreational fisheries management issues in science needs assessments for the National Marine Sanctuary System.
- Assess the utility of angler reported electronic data as a supplement to existing data collections.
- Promote improved recreational fisheries data collection and reporting for shared resources within international management bodies, and enhance management of such fisheries where needed.
- Identify avenues to engage recreational fishermen in habitat research, such as through community monitoring groups or cooperative research on habitat issues such as limitations to recreational fish productivity.

COMMUNICATE AND ENGAGE WITH THE RECREATIONAL FISHING PUBLIC

One of NOAA Fisheries' most important responsibilities is to involve interested members of the public in our fact-finding, evaluation, and decision-making processes. Industry, anglers, and others are affected by these actions and decisions and want to have a voice in shaping outcomes. It is important to ensure that interested stakeholders have the opportunity to contribute to the science and decision-making in a meaningful way. An engaged and informed constituency results in better science, decision-making, and buy-in, which facilitates effective solutions that make the best use of taxpayer dollars and best serve the public. Actions supporting this guiding principle include:

Listen, respond, and seek to improve understanding.

- Create formal and informal opportunities to communicate with anglers and gain feedback about messages, products, and channels of distribution. Seek to better understand what anglers want to know and how they would prefer to receive that information. This will include hosting bi-annual webinars with the recreational community and attending major community events.
- Increase the amount of content (e.g., feature stories, videos, alerts) relevant to anglers.

- Make information more readily available by tapping into new and existing resources for distributing content (e.g., social media, fishing publications) and creating new partnerships (e.g., with states, fishing organizations).
- Maintain strong working relationships and open lines of communication with community leaders to ensure regular dialogue and a policy of "no surprises."
- Work with interested stakeholder groups to host regular roundtable discussions in each region to strengthen relationships and share information.

Provide opportunities for meaningful engagement.

- Identify opportunities for angler engagement in major NOAA Fisheries actions and decision-making that affect recreational fishing.
- Improve coordination with NOAA's Office of National Marine Sanctuaries to increase angler participation in marine protected resources regulatory processes and data collection opportunities.
- Utilize the full suite of available tools (e.g., webinars, in-person meetings, online comments) to provide opportunities for all who wish to engage.
- Follow up with anglers about resulting agency actions or decisions.

Provide relevant NOAA information in an efficient and consistent manner.

- Test and implement mobile platforms as a way to communicate fishery regulations.
- Improve coordination among NOAA line offices by strengthening relationships and improving communication processes.
- Pull together NOAA Fisheries staff and our state and Council partners to create recreational fishing data communications teams in each region to improve stakeholder understanding and access to catch and effort information.
- Strengthen internal communication and outreach capacity by providing training to regional recreational fisheries coordinators.

In: Recreational Fisheries in the U.S.
Editor: Ellen K. Parker

ISBN: 978-1-63485-595-2
© 2016 Nova Science Publishers, Inc.

Chapter 3

RECREATIONAL FISHERIES YEAR IN REVIEW 2012[*]

National Marine Fisheries Service

LETTER FROM ASSISTANT ADMINISTRATOR FOR FISHERIES

April 2013

Recreational Fishers

NOAA recognizes the important role anglers play as stewards of our marine resources, contributors to our coastal economies, and in enriching the lives of millions of Americans. It is rewarding to see our relationships with the recreational fishing community improving as we move forward, working together.

The many actions we have taken since 2010 under the Recreational Fisheries Engagement Initiative are making a difference, and as we report in this Recreational Fisheries Engagement Initiative 2012 Update, we continue to make progress. Nearly 80 percent of the National Action Agenda is complete or well underway. However, even as we see progress through our work

---

[*] This is an edited, reformatted and augmented version of a publication issued by the National Oceanic and Atmospheric Administration, April 2013.

together *and* improvements in fish stocks as we execute plans to end overfishing and rebuild depleted stocks, I recognize our work is far from finished. This is especially true with the complex and longstanding challenges related to data quality and allocation, and with the needs to sustain and increase access to rebuilding stocks.

We recognize these issues remain as priorities for fishermen, and they do for NOAA as well. We are committed to working through our scientific, management and public engagement processes to continue addressing these issues. I appreciate and remain encouraged by the recreational community's continued engagement and willingness to work with us to address these and other challenges.

The Engagement Initiative is creating positive momentum. While many changes are incremental, with sustained attention, change is becoming more obvious. I am confident that the positive outcomes of our collective, focused attention will increase as we continue forward together. I am a firm believer in collaboration, and sustainably managing our common ocean resources is a job best accomplished in a partnership. Thank you for all your ideas and cooperation in 2012, I look forward to continuing our work with you in 2013.

Sincerely,

Eric Schwaab
Assistant Administrator for Fisheries,
performing the functions and duties
of the Assistant Secretary for Conservation and Management

RECREATIONAL FISHERIES ENGAGEMENT INITIATIVE 2012 UPDATE

Three years have passed since NOAA embarked on the Recreational Fisheries Engagement Initiative— a focused effort to establish stronger and more trusting relationship with the recreational fishing community. The Engagement Initiative is about listening to anglers, taking action to address critical issues of concern, following through on commitments, and empowering anglers to be responsible stewards and resource users.

Ideas provided by anglers at the 2010 Saltwater Recreational Fishing Summit and since have resulted in specific tasks outlined in the national and subsequent regional Action Agendas. These planning documents serve as our annual activities roadmap.

With the guidance and input of the recreational fishing community, we have fulfilled many of the Action Agendas' commitments and are making substantial progress on the rest. This document takes stock of the important steps taken by NOAA Fisheries to act on key issues of concern, strengthen ties with the recreational fishing community, encourage participation in the management process, and ensure a satisfying recreational fishing experience today and for generations of anglers to come.

Team Approach

Recreational fisheries issues are a critical factor in our day-to-day considerations and decisions. Our partnerships have been vital to the progress we have made thus far. However, to be fully successful, we need the continued support of anglers in these efforts, including conservation action on the water, constructive input, guidance, and feedback.

NOAA has adopted a team approach to engage on recreational activities, both externally and internally. NOAA Fisheries' National Policy Advisor for Recreational Fisheries coordinates these efforts. The National Policy Advisor provides input on all recreational issues directly to the Assistant Administrator and the NOAA Fisheries Leadership Council, where the Agency's senior decision makers provide longterm policy, programmatic, and budgetary advice.

The Marine Fisheries Advisory Committee (MAFAC) and its Recreational Fisheries Working Group serve as a critical resource to the agency. This group of fishermen and conservation and industry leaders provides seasoned input on a wide variety of topics from an array of national, regional and sector perspectives. NOAA Fisheries' team of regional recreational coordinators—often the face of NOAA Fisheries to their region's fishermen—is responsible for much of the on-the-ground progress in the Engagement Initiative. The regional coordinators provide feedback to NOAA Fisheries leadership on key recreational fishing issues in their region, allowing the agency to more effectively address national recreational challenges.

NOAA Fisheries National program offices, including Sustainable Fisheries, Habitat Conservation, Protected Resources, Science and

Technology, and Communications are active participants in Engagement Initiative efforts and have committed staff to support the engagement initiative.

Building Trust

We have worked to improve the relationship between NOAA and the angling community through improving communication, following through in commitments, and maintaining a sustained focus on the priorities of anglers. Creating a stronger relationship requires perseverance, dedication, and an ongoing commitment to work together. Such efforts are difficult to quantify in the short term, but are fundamental to creating lasting change.

One marker of change is a strengthened recreational fisheries perspective in the NOAA and NOAA Fisheries planning processes, ranging from the broad NOAA Next Generation Strategic Plan down to the focused NOAA Fisheries Regional Action Agendas.

Taking Action

Sustainably managing our common ocean resources is a job best accomplished in partnership. The Recreational Saltwater Fishing Summit sought to strengthen the important relationship between NOAA Fisheries and the recreational fishing community. With more than 100 participants from across the nation, the Summit focused attention on the most pressing issues facing our recreational fisheries, including the quality and timeliness of recreational catch and effort data, concerns over catch shares, and recreational representation in the management process. Equally important, Summit participants told us that follow-through would be the critical measure of success.

Importance of Recreational Fishing

NOAA Fisheries appreciates that recreational fishing is part of the history and fabric of our nation and wants to continue to improve upon this great tradition. Fishing has always been an important social activity promoting stronger families and communities, providing both employment and a way of life for many, and serving as a large economic driver at all levels—locally, regionally, and nationally.

Recent estimates indicate there are approximately 12 million saltwater recreational anglers taking about 85 million trips a year. Combined, expenditures total $31 billion dollars, representing an $82 billion dollar impact and supporting half a million jobs.

Just as important is the legacy of recreational fishermen as conservationists concerned about the health and sustainability of the marine environment. By practicing catch and release techniques, advocating for and participating in the development of better fisheries data and science, improving habitat, and engaging in the policy process, recreational anglers continue to effect positive change and ensure their voice is heard.

The 2010 Recreational Saltwater Fishing Action Agenda described NOAA's path forward in response to the ideas expressed by Summit participants. It identified a number of preliminary engagement actions and continues to serve as our roadmap for efforts to address priorities and concerns identified by leading members of the recreational fishing community.

The updates below highlight our steady progress. Some efforts, such as the FishSmart workshops, are highly visible and result in immediate benefits to the community at large. Others, such as our internal work to include recreational fishing issues in policy discussions at all levels, are less visible outside NOAA, but equally far-reaching and important to the future of fishing.

Highlights

Greater Regional Engagement. In December 2011, we released Regional Action Agendas for each NOAA Fisheries region and for Atlantic Highly Migratory Species. Each agenda was prepared by regional NOAA Fisheries staff in consultation with members of MAFAC's Recreational Fisheries Working Group and other members of the fishing public. Each agenda is individually tailored to address the priorities and issues expressed by regional recreational stakeholders and focuses on measurable actions that can be achieved within the year.

Some of the regional highlights during 2012 included:

- Hiring a full-time recreational fisheries coordinator and convening a regional recreational fishing summit (Pacific Islands).
- Conducting thresher shark hooking mortality research in cooperation with outside scientists and recreational fishermen (Southwest Region).
- Implementing recreational web pages and other communications tools in regional offices to provide anglers with up-to-date information.
- Collaborating with anglers to host a series of workshops to improve survival of recreationally released fish.

NOAA Fisheries is again working with constituents to update the regional Action Agendas in 2013. Please see Appendix A for a detailed summary of on-the-ground progress in each region.

Improved Data. Quality data must be the basis for our shared understanding of the status of stocks and informed decision-making, and anglers identified this as a top priority. NOAA Fisheries actively engaged in numerous collaborative projects with the community aimed at providing improved biological, social, and economic information including:

Supporting the Marine Recreational Information Program's (MRIP) efforts to improve how recreational data are collected and reported. A major milestone was implementation of an improved method for calculating catch estimates in early 2012. This improved method removed sampling bias, resulting in more accurate estimates. Other notable progress included:

- Completion of an electronic logbook pilot program in the Gulf of Mexico for-hire fleet; study results are being finalized.
- Assessment of a catch card program to monitor recreational billfish landings in Puerto Rico; Building on what was learned in Puerto Rico, NOAA Fisheries is currently conducting a pilot catch card study of bluefin tuna landings in Massachusetts.
- Review of sampling and estimation designs for recreational data collection programs in California, Oregon, and Washington.
- Securing additional funding to increase the quantity and quality of stock assessments across the nation, with particular focus in South Atlantic and Gulf of Mexico.
- Fielding a National Angler Expenditure Survey to document recreational fishing's economic contribution to the nation.

More Fish Today and Tomorrow

After years of hard work and real sacrifice, benefits are beginning to accrue as stocks recover. In 2012, the number of fish stocks considered overfished or subject to overfishing declined, to 19% (41) and 10% (41) of assessed stocks, respectively. Six stocks were declared newly rebuilt, including Coho salmon in the Strait of Juan de Fuca.

Augmenting these conservation gains is NOAA Fisheries' work with FishSmart, an angler-led, NOAA funded effort to enhance fisheries by improving the survival of recreationally released fish. Through a series of science-based regional workshops involving the angling community, Fishery Management Councils (Councils), researchers, non-governmental organizations, and federal and state government agencies, participants generated research and management recommendations and angling best-practices. The workshops promoted development of new fish-friendly gears as well as widespread Council discussion of release mortality issues. NOAA Fisheries is now focusing on coordinating and refining the agency's scientific efforts regarding recreational release mortality. We are confident that this joint government–angler effort is the next step in the evolution of better ensuring the survival of released fish, enhancing time on the water for recreational anglers.

More Fishing Opportunities. We hear from many anglers about the importance of protecting and enhancing fishing opportunities. Based on questions or comments from anglers, NOAA Fisheries:

- Partnered with anglers and NOAA's National Ocean Service on the 2012 Sanctuaries Classic fishing tournament, a nationwide effort to encourage recreational fishing within NOAA's system of National Marine Sanctuaries.
- Initiated scoping on National Standard 1 to explore the concerns of anglers and others regarding implementation of annual catch limits and accountability measures, among other issues.
- Worked closely with the Councils to promote more adaptive management to allow for increased fishing opportunities, including:
  - Opening the South Atlantic red snapper fishery in September 2012.
  - Extending the 2012 Gulf red snapper season to account for poor weather conditions.

- Providing additional red snapper allocation to the recreational sector in 2011 and 2012; and adjusting the 2010 fishing season to minimize the effects of the Deepwater Horizon oil spill.
- Initiating an amendment to address allocation issues in the Mid-Atlantic scup fishery.
- Opened the door to addressing allocation by commissioning an in-depth review of allocation issues (released Jan. 2013); produced a technical memorandum reviewing historic allocation decisions; and addressed allocation in the National Catch Share Policy by recommending all fishery management programs re-visit allocation on a regular basis. NOAA is now working with the Councils to develop a path forward.
- Engaged fishermen, scientists, and government agencies on the issue of oil platform removals in the Gulf of Mexico which contributed to a rapid and broad interagency effort to produce comprehensive federal Frequently Asked Questions (FAQs) on the issue, providing a common understanding of the facts on the water. NOAA continues to build an enhanced understanding among and between federal agencies and constituents on the issue.

Approximately 80 percent of the National Action Agenda is completed or seeing significant progress, but our work is far from finished. Important priorities, most notably catch and effort data collection and quota allocation, need continued attention and remain as Agency priorities. Further, continued focus on how to maximize fishing opportunities associated with rebuilding stocks remains a high priority. As catch rates increase, new management approaches will be required to sustain fishing seasons and time on the water for recreational anglers. NOAA Fisheries is encouraged by and appreciative of the community's continued engagement and willingness to work cooperatively with the Agency toward better managed, more productive, and more satisfying fisheries.

The Engagement Initiative is creating positive change and momentum, one step at a time. While some of the improvements may be small, these critical first steps provide the foundation for achieving our long-term goals. The impact of our collective, focused attention will grow as we continue to take these steps together.

2013 Priorities

In 2013, we will continue advancing our existing commitments outlined in the Action Agendas, while also laying the groundwork for the next generation of regional and national plans.

Specifically, we will:

1. Improve how NOAA collects and reports recreational fishing information by implementing a new method for collecting data from anglers and releasing results from the angler expenditure survey.
2. Continue to work toward recreational fishing experiences that reflect the needs and desires of the recreational community. We'll begin by undertaking new human dimension research, and responding to a new NOAA-funded report on allocation.
3. Fulfill NOAA's promises to make a difference at the regional and local levels through the continued implementation of regional action agendas, regular town-hall conference calls with regional leadership, and at least one constituent meeting in each region.
4. Identify opportunities for community engagement in fisheries policy discussions, such as participation in the Managing Our Nation's Fisheries III conference (May 2013) and regional roundtable discussions (Winter/Spring 2013).
5. Help anglers become better marine stewards by providing science-based information on barotrauma and catch and release techniques through the next phase of FishSmart.
6. Continue to strengthen science through the application of cutting edge stock assessment techniques, and improve survey data collection using advanced technologies and alternative survey platforms, and improved collection methodologies.

Conclusion

As demand for our ocean resources continues to increase, the importance of accurate information, sound decision-making, honest conversation, and collective action will also grow. Our commitment to action and trust-building through the Recreational Fisheries Engagement Initiative will help us meet these challenges.

REGIONAL UPDATE: NORTHEAST

Goal	Objective	Project(S)	Results
Improve Recreational Fishing Opportunities	Reduce user conflicts on artificial reefs in Federal waters.	Special Management Zones (SMZs) for sportfish funded artificial reefs.	Participated in the Mid-Atlantic Fishery Management Council (Council) Special Management Zones (SMZ) process to provide data and ensure the recreational perspective was integrated into planning. The Council has developed several options for 5 proposed SMZs that are being taken to public hearings in 2013.
	Ensure that proposals to allocate scup fully consider the needs of all stakeholders.	Evaluate recreational/ commercial allocation in the scup fishery under the Mid-Atlantic Fishery Management Council process.	Provided an evaluation of scup allocations to the Council management for consideration.
	Ensure recreational allocation of Atlantic mackerel.	Provide for a recreational allocation in the Atlantic mackerel fishery.	Implemented a recreational allocation through Amendment 13 to the Atlantic Squid, Mackerel, and Butterfish Fishery Management Plan.
	Increase spawning and nursery area for anadromous species.	Improve fish passage for the Saco River, ME, and Hudson River, NY.	Undertook consultations on Federal Actions to improve Essential Fish Habitat (EFH) for Atlantic salmon, striped bass, shad, and other species.
		Dam removal and fish passage projects in the Northeast Region.	In late 2011 through 2012, the Northeast Restoration Center completed 10 of the 15 anticipated dam removal and fish passage projects, began construction on two of the projects, and continued the planning and design of the remaining three projects.
	Protect important recreational fish habitat.	Improve Essential Fish Habitat designations and review of areas of high habitat vulnerability.	Provided technical assistance to both the New England and Mid-Atlantic Fishery Management Councils for EFH on all major fisheries regulatory actions. Work groups and initial review of data for designation of areas of high habitat vulnerability have begun.
	Prevent overfishing on recreational fish stocks.	Protect recreational fish stocks by instituting Annual Catch Limits/ Accountability Measures to prevent	Annual catch limits (ACLs) and Accountability Measures (AMs) are in place for all federally managed stocks in the northeast, except squid species that are exempt from ACLs and /AMs because of their short life span.

Recreational Fisheries Year in Review 2012

Goal	Objective	Project(S)	Results
		overfishing.	
	Protect forage species and monitor and reduce bycatch of recreational species.	Protect forage species and monitor and reduce bycatch of species important to the recreational fishing community.	Annual specifications for Atlantic herring and Atlantic mackerel have taken into account recreational fisheries and forage issues. Amendment 13 to the Atlantic mackerel established a recreational catch limit that was higher than recent reported landings. In cooperation with the New England Council, began development of Amendment 14 to the Mackerel, squid, butterfish, and Amendment 5 to the Atlantic Herring Fishery Management Plans to maintain forge base fish populations.
	Reduce negative impacts of proposed projects on fish habitat.	Improve habitat protections through consultation with Federal agencies proposing to impact EFH and other living marine resources.	Participated in Bureau of Ocean Energy Management (BOEM) Offshore Renewable Energy Task Forces in Maine, Massachusetts, Rhode Island, New York, New Jersey, Delaware, Maryland and Virginia. Provided technical guidance on the development of Wind Energy Areas, and comments on BOEM's Site Assessment and Leasing actions throughout the Northeast.
	Meet NOAA's regulatory responsibilities for managing recreational species under the Magnuson-Stevens Act.	Summer flounder, scup, black sea bass, and bluefish annual recreational fishing specifications and Northeast groundfish (cod, haddock, pollack etc.) regulations.	Monitored status of the stocks and fisheries for these species and annual management measures have been implemented in cooperation with the Mid-Atlantic Fishery Management Council, and Atlantic States Marine Fisheries Commission (ASMFC) and with the New England Fishery Management Council for Northeast groundfish.
Improve Recreational Catch, Effort, and Status Data	Provide a more timely and efficient reporting system to party/ charter vessels.	Implement electronic logbook reporting by for-hire vessels.	The option for expanded electronic logbook reporting for groundfish recreational party/charterboats was made available. Also, northeast party/charter vessels can now send in required "did not fish" reports through the northeast electronic fish-on-line reporting program.
	Design a project that will involve party/charter vessels in cooperative research.	Host a workshop on fixed-gear survey techniques and the potential to conduct a cooperative research party/ charter marine recreational based	The workshop was held in Narragansett, RI, on July 12–13 2011. The Northeast Fisheries Science Center (NEFSC) is pursuing other means to fund this project.

Regional Update: Northeast (Continued)

Goal	Objective	Project(S)	Results
		survey.	
	Keep users of MRIP data informed of program updates and changes.	Create a Northeast MRIP user group.	Created a Northeast MRIP user group and have begun annual meetings. A coordination group to look into improved integration of the Northeast charter/ party boat recreational log book and MRIP For-Hire data collection programs has been formed.
	Provide advice and information on data needs for the management of Federal recreational fishing programs.	Atlantic Coast Cooperative Statistics Program Recreational Fisheries Technical Committee.	Supported recreational data outreach efforts, and participated on the Atlantic Coast Cooperative Statistics Program Recreational Fisheries Technical Committee.
	Provide the scientific information necessary to assess and manage recreational fish stocks.	Survey and research to understand the biology and stock dynamics of important species supporting marine recreational fisheries.	Conducted the Northeast spring and fall fish trawl surveys, the cooperative research Northeast Area Monitoring Program trawl survey, and have implemented a black sea bass cooperative research stock monitoring survey, and a cooperative research back sea bass tagging study of New Jersey.
	Produce accurate stock status assessments for recreational fish stocks.	Conduct improved stock assessments for black sea bass, Gulf of Maine cod, and three stocks of winter flounder.	Completed the stock assessments and these data were the basis for 2012 catch limits. Additionally an Atlantic cod discard mortality workshop was held that gathered input from fishermen (including recreational fisheries representatives) and scientists.
	Give priority to conducting stock assessments on the recreational fish stocks with the most important immediate needs.	Prioritize stock assessments for important recreational stocks.	Annual updates were scheduled for bluefish, summer flounder, scup, and black sea bass, and groundfish stocks (cod, haddock, pollock, winter, and yellowtail flounder) in 2012. New assessments or stock updates scheduled for 2014 are striped bass, bluefish, summer flounder, scup, and black sea bass, Georges Bank cod and haddock, and tilefish.
Improve Social and Economic Data	Obtain improved economic information on party/charter recreational fishing boats.	Complete a For-Hire cost/ earnings survey in the northeast region.	Finalized a report on economic information related to Northeast party/charter boats in late 2011 and result was distributed in 2012.
	Obtain improved	Valuation and	Constructed an economic model to

Goal	Objective	Project(S)	Results
	economic information on the recreational groundfish fishery.	economic impact study of recreational anglers in the Northeast region.	estimate the effects of regulatory changes on total angler effort for the groundfish fishery in 2010/2011. The modeling program was used in 2012 to estimate how proposed management changes could affect fishing mortality, angler effort, and the value anglers obtain from their fishing experience.
	Provide economic information on the recreational fishery to allow for informed management decisions.	Valuation and economic impact study of recreational summer flounder, black sea bass, and scup anglers in the northeast region.	Developed an economic model to estimate the effects of regulatory changes on angler effort, fishing mortality, and angler value for summer flounder, black sea bass, and scup fisheries in 2010/2011. The modeling program may be used in 2013 to help better understand the effects of proposed regulatory changes.
	Estimation of the "true" value of marine saltwater licenses in Massachusetts.	Measure the economic value of saltwater fishing licenses in Massachusetts.	Conducted a valuation survey of recreational anglers in Massachusetts. Analysis of the collected data is ongoing. Study results will be reported in 2013.
Improve Social and Economic Data	Provide for an accurate and precise recreational use survey.	2011/2012 National Marine Recreational Use Survey.	Contributed expertise for the design of the 2011/2012 National Marine Recreational Use Survey, and developed a recreational fisheries management decision support model.
	Improve awareness and understanding of NOAA decisions and activities affecting recreational fishing through web-based information.	Develop recreational fishing web pages.	Built a regional recreational fishing web page, and access to it was placed on the front page of the Northeast Regional Office (NERO) web site.
Improve Communications	Direct interaction of NERO/NEFSC leadership with the recreational fisheries community.	Host a Northeast Region annual recreational fisheries forum.	The annual recreational fisheries forum was deferred due to 2012 pending Northeast Region and Science Center leadership changes. It will be replaced by a Northeast Recreational Fisheries Information meeting in 2013.
	Obtain direct sub-regional feedback on the action agenda.	Host Sub-regional Northeast region recreational fisheries information meetings.	The Sub-regional Northeast Region recreational fisheries information meetings were deferred due to 2012 pending Northeast Region and Science Center leadership changes. They will be replaced by 2 Northeast Recreational Fisheries Informational region-wide town hall calls in 2013

Regional Update: Northeast (Continued)

Goal	Objective	Project(S)	Results
	Facilitate Information flow on recreational fishing data collection programs.	Support MRIP outreach and information activities within the Northeast region.	Gave a NERO internal recreational fisheries lecture describing MRIP activities to improve northeast recreational fisheries data collection, MRIP materials were passed out at recreational fishing outreach events, NERO staff assisted MRIP on planning a New England MRIP outreach road trip, and a northeast MRIP users meeting was held to improve communication among MRIP, Northeast Region, state and fishery management council personnel.
	Generate goodwill within the recreational fishing community by improving information flow to recreational fishing associations and clubs.	Develop an email list of Northeast recreational fishing associations and clubs.	Created an e-mail list-serve of recreational constituents. The list serve was used several times a quarter to send out key regulatory changes or announcements of high interest to the recreational fisheries community.
	Direct communication with the fishing and boating public.	Special outreach at recreational fishing/ boating events.	NOAA Fisheries staff have attended eight club, association, or fishing/boating events.
	Provide information to the recreational fisheries community on how to identify and release sturgeon.	Sturgeon identification and release brochure.	Developed an informative sticker to identify and correctly release sturgeon, rather than a brochure. Over 2,500 have been distributed to anglers near likely areas for sturgeon interactions. The remaining stickers will be distributed a fishing shows and/or tackle/bait shops in 2013.
	Inform the recreational fishery community about marine aquaculture issues.	Educate and solicit input from recreational fishing groups on aquaculture.	Developed and distributed an aquaculture brochure.
	Inform the recreational fisheries community about the Atlantic Coastal Fish Habitat Partnership.	Atlantic Coastal Fish Habitat Partnership Outreach.	No action on this was taken in 2012.

Recreational Fisheries Year in Review 2012

Goal	Objective	Project(S)	Results
	Develop Habitat Information Pamphlet.	Inform the recreational fisheries community on the importance of protecting marine habitat to maintain healthy fisheries.	Developed a pamphlet on the importance of protecting marine habitat, with information on how to set up a fishing line recycling program.
Institutional Orientation	NOAA Fisheries regional personnel to be aware of the importance of the Action Agenda.	Conduct in-house recreational fisheries Action Agenda awareness meetings.	Gave an internal lecture on recreational fisheries issues including the action agenda to Regional Office staff. Regional Office leadership and division leadership were briefed on the action agenda.
	Improve communication between the USFWS and the NOAA Fisheries Northeast Region regarding marine fisheries grant funding programs.	Hold a NOAA Fisheries and U.S. Fish and Wildlife Service Northeast grants workshop to review grants that support recreational fishing.	It is planned that this action be repeated every 2 years. The next workshop will be conducted in 2014.
	Improve the understanding of the federal marine fishery management process by the recreational fishing community.	Give an in-house lecture on recreational fishing issues, science, and management.	Due to the success of this item. Annual lectures of this nature will be planned for 2013 and 2014.
	Inform other NOAA entities of the Action Agenda and partner with them to provide information on NOAA services and products to the recreational fishing community.	Coordinate recreational fishing outreach activities with the Stellwagen Bank National Marine Sanctuary.	Shared outreach materials from the Stellwagen Bank Sanctuary as part of Northeast Region activities at fishing shows. The Northeast Recreational Coordinator briefed sanctuary staff, and the NOAA North Atlantic Coordination Team on the Action Agenda.

REGIONAL UPDATE: SOUTHEAST

Goal	Objective	Project(S)	Results
Improve Recreational Fishing Opportunities	Extend Gulf of Mexico Red Snapper Fishery.	Reopen the recreational fisheries when excess quota is available, and work closely with the Gulf FMC to evaluate alternate seasons.	Extended Gulf of Mexico recreational red snapper fishing season six days in mid-July 2012 because severe weather reduced opportunity to fish during the pre-specified 40-day season. Preliminary data indicate the recreational fishery exceeded its catch limit by about 40 percent, which will be taken into account when setting limits for the 2013 season.
	Maximize recreational fishing opportunities while maintaining conservation objectives in the South Atlantic.	Provide recreational fishermen opportunities to target South Atlantic red snapper if sustainable.	Provided recreational fishermen two opportunities to target South Atlantic red snapper during three-day weekend openings in 2012, and supported South Atlantic Council action to develop a methodology to specify appropriate catch limits in future years based on discard and rebuilding data. Recreational fishermen targeted red snapper in the South Atlantic for the first time in over two years. NOAA Fisheries is currently reviewing the Council's proposed methodology for calculating future catch limits which, if approved, could lead to another reopening in summer or fall of 2013.
	Improve timeliness of management responses to data.	Respond quickly to new scientific information supporting annual catch limit increases.	Implemented the South Atlantic Council's proposed catch limit increase for golden tilefish and supported South Atlantic and Gulf Council action to increase catch limits of yellowtail snapper and Gulf of Mexico gag. NOAA Fisheries is currently reviewing the Councils' proposed increases for yellowtail snapper and Gulf of Mexico gag.
	Ensure regulatory measures minimize adverse impacts to extent possible.	Support Gulf Council action to further minimize the impact of shallow-water grouper accountability measures on harvest while still maintaining conservation objectives.	NOAA Fisheries is currently reviewing this Council action which, if approved, will expand recreational fishing opportunities in 2013.
	Enlist recreational community in	Approve an exempted fishing	Approved an exempted fishing permit allowing recreational tournaments in the

Recreational Fisheries Year in Review 2012

Goal	Objective	Project(S)	Results
	improving data.	permit allowing recreational tournaments in the five Gulf Coast states to harvest red snapper for scientific purposes.	five Gulf Coast states to harvest red snapper for scientific purposes after the close of the recreational red snapper season. These tournaments provided anglers the opportunity to help fishery scientist collect biological information on red snapper outside the normal season. The information collected during these tournaments will be used to further understand the age structure and reproductive status of red snapper in the Gulf of Mexico.
	Improve fishing flexibility within the for-hire industry.	Gulf Advisory Panels.	Received a request for a headboat cooperative EFP, which is under review.
Improve Recreational Catch, Effort, and Status Data	Evaluate Alternative data collection systems to improve timeliness of for-hire data.	Complete pilot Projects testing electronic logbook reporting on headboats in the South Atlantic and charter boats in the Gulf of Mexico.	These completed projects provide data and information to help fishery Scientists and managers better understand the benefits and limitations of electronic reporting.
	Implement an electronic logbook pilot program to improve catch and effort data for the for-hire fleet in the Gulf of Mexico.	Electronic logbook program	As of Jan1, 2013, the Southeast Region Headboat Survey (SRHS) started collecting logbook data electronically in the U.S. south Atlantic and Gulf of Mexico. Headboat captains now have the ability to submit trip reports through a secure website and mobile app by using their personal computers, tablets, or smart phones.
	Better understand recreational fishery interactions with protected resources.	Implement pilot survey in South Atlantic to obtain information on sea turtle interactions in recreational fisheries in collaboration with the Marine Recreational Information Program.	This pilot project will help us to determine the feasibility of expanding the survey throughout the Southeast Region to better estimate and minimize sea turtle interactions in recreational fisheries.
Improve Recreational Catch, Effort, and Status Data	Improve understanding of recreational catch and effort in the	Participate in marine recreational sampling	The USVI workshop outcomes will guide the development of a sampling survey design for those islands. The Puerto Rico workshop considered pilot project design

Regional Update: Southeast (Continued)

Goal	Objective	Project(S)	Results
	U.S. Caribbean.	workshops in the USVI and Puerto Rico.	for adding queen conch and spiny lobster to the recreational harvest survey.
Improve Recreational Catch, Effort, and Status Data	Create a fishery-independent survey in the U.S. South Atlantic to index the abundance of red snapper and other reef fishes.	South East Fishery-Independent Survey.	Continued the SouthEast Fishery Independent Survey created in 2010 in collaboration with the Marine Resource, Assessment and Prediction program to improve reef fish sampling in the U.S. South Atlantic.
	Determine the frequency and extent of bottlenose dolphin interactions with recreational fishing gear and the impact these interactions have on bottlenose dolphins.	Development of survey on bottlenose dolphin-recreational fishery interactions.	Developed survey questions on dolphin-recreational fishery interactions to add on to the redesigned MRIP survey and are in communication with MRIP about next steps. Also received the final report of a 2-year research project in the northern Gulf of Mexico in which for-hire captains were employed to help assess/characterize the frequency of occurrence and geographic scope of depredation by bottlenose dolphins on recreational fishing gear and to develop preventative measures to reduce/eliminate interactions.
Improve Social and Economic Data	Improve understanding of the impact and value of recreational fisheries.	Conduct analysis evaluating economic efficiency of current commercial and recreational allocations for Gulf of Mexico red grouper, gag, black grouper and red snapper.	These completed analyses will inform Gulf Council deliberations on potential allocation adjustments.
	Improve the understanding of human dimensions of recreational fishing.	Improve the understanding of human dimensions of recreational fishing.	Socio-economic studies were completed to better understand sport fishing demand, angler value and cost\earnings in the in the South Atlantic and Gulf of Mexico recreational fisheries. The final reports include: Holland et al. 2012. "The Operations and Economics of the For-Hire Fishing Fleets of the South Atlantic States and the Atlantic Coast of Florida"
			Savolainen et al. 2012. "Economic and Atitudinal Perspectives of the Recreational For-hire Fishing Industry in the U.S. Gulf

Goal	Objective	Project(S)	Results
			of Mexico"
			Carter, D. W. and C. Liese. 2012. The Economic Value of Catching and Keeping or Releasing Saltwater Sport Fish in the Southeast USA. North American Journal of Fisheries Management 32(4): 613-25.
Improve Communications	Educate the media about marine conservation issues.	Participate in Theodore Roosevelt Conservation Partnership Saltwater Media Summit at Mote Marine Laboratory in Sarasota, Florida.	Southeast Regional Administrator and Recreational Fishing Coordinator participated. This meeting provided fishermen and fishery managers the opportunity to engage the media on marine conservation issues.
	Provide regular opportunities for informal public question and answer sessions with the Regional Administrator and Science Center Director.	Host evening question and answer sessions for interested constituents at all Gulf of Mexico and South Atlantic Fishery Management Council meetings.	Southeast Regional Administrator and Southeast Science Center Director hosted informal discussions which enable NOAA Fisheries leadership to be knowledgeable about and responsive to constituent concerns.
	Educate recreational fishermen about the fishery science and management process.	Engage the Steering Committee for the Marine Resource Education Program.	Recreational Fisheries Coordinator served on the Planning Committee. This Committee developed agenda and speaker recommendations for science and management workshops to be held in 2013.
	Meet with constituent groups about recreational fisheries issues.	Constituent Issues.	Met with recreational organizations upon request, including American Sportfishing Association, Coastal Conservation Association, Clearwater Marine Association, Gulf of Mexico Charter Fisherman's Association, and the Orange Beach Fishing Association.
Improve Communications	Expand engagement of the recreational fishing community in data collection programs.	Expand engagement of the recreational fishing community in data collection programs.	The Adopt-A-Billfish program enlists the help of billfish anglers in tagging operations throughout the Atlantic Ocean, Caribbean Sea, Bahamas and Bermuda. As part of this program, scientists maintain an Atlantic-wide constituent-based cooperative tagging program (Cooperative Tagging Center), as well as conduct electronic tagging of billfish using pop-up satellite archival tag (PSAT) technology. The Cooperative Tagging Center works in

Regional Update: Southeast (Continued)

Goal	Objective	Project(S)	Results
			collaboration with NOAA Fisheries Service's SEFSC and Southwest Fisheries Science Center, University of Miami Center for Sustainable Fisheries, The Billfish Foundation, the Bermuda Department of Environmental Protection, and the International Game Fish Association.
	Improve communications with the recreational fishing industry on the issue of bottlenose dolphin inter-actions with recreational fishing gear.	Improve communications with the recreational fishing industry on the issue of bottlenose dolphin interactions with recreational fishing gear.	Sent targeted mailings of educational materials and letters to areas where there are documented entanglements and rescues. Outreach materials are geared toward providing information on how fishermen and the public can help prevent these interactions and steps to take when an interaction may occur (e.g., reporting). Our bottlenose dolphin experts also participated in the first FishSmart workshop April 11–13 on Gulf of Mexico and South Atlantic fisheries, where workshop attendees discussed best angler practices, equipment ideas, provided guidance to management bodies, and identified gaps in current scientific knowledge about safe catch-and-release techniques.
Institutional Orientation	Reduce discards and discard mortality.	Engage in FishSmart activities.	Participated in Southeast FishSmart Barotrauma Workshop April 11–13 at Florida Fish and Wildlife Conservation Commission's research facility in St. Petersburg, Florida. This workshop educated fishery managers, scientists and anglers about methods to reduce discards and discard mortality.
	Improve understanding of the stock assessment process i.e., SEDAR.	Provide an opportunity for stock assessment scientists, data collectors, fisheries researchers, and constituents to take part in the stock assessment and to collectively develop and review complex fisheries stock assessment analyses.	Participation of recreational constituents in the assessment process.

Goal	Objective	Project(S)	Results
	Improve understanding of the federal fishery management process.	Marine Resource Education Program.	Assembled an executive steering committee consisting of NMFS and Council staff, fishing constituents and other experts in the field of fisheries management and research to plan the curriculums for science and management workshops to be held in 2013. The science workshop will be held April 2–4 in St. Petersburg, Florida. The management workshop has not yet been scheduled but will take place later this fall.
	Define recreational allocation in Puerto Rico.	Caribbean Fishery Management Council and NOAA Fisheries Service are working together on amendments to implement separate recreational and commercial catch limits.	Specified separate annual catch limits for commercial and recreational fisheries in Puerto Rico.

REGIONAL UPDATE: ATLANTIC HIGHLY MIGRATORY SPECIES

Goal	Objective	Project(S)	Results
Improve Recreational Fishing Opportunities	Provide fair and/or equitable access to recreational Atlantic HMS fisheries as consistent with legal obligations, stock health, and	Continue to provide fair and equitable access to recreational Atlantic HMS fisheries.	Atlantic HMS fisheries remain viable and very popular. Tournament registration years. Approximately 25,000 Recreational and 4,000 Charter/Headboat permits were issued in 2012.
	the goals and objectives of relevant fishery management plans.		

Regional Update: Atlantic Highly Migratory Species (Continued)

Goal	Objective	Project(S)	Results
	Provide for, and improve where practical, recreational opportunities for Atlantic HMS through management practices that ensure healthy stocks are available to the fishery.	Consider opportunities to increase access to the swordfish fishery that result in minimal bycatch of protected resources and non-target species. Educate constituents about the inclusion of roundscale spearfish in the Atlantic HMS management unit with management measures identical to white marlin. ICCAT Negotiations. Provide for recreational opportunities to catch Atlantic tunas. Support recreational fishing opportunities to catch sharks.	Total U.S. swordfish landings through November 2012 are about 40% higher than the average for the same period from 2009–2011. Outreach materials including the Atlantic HMS Recreational Compliance Guide have been distributed to the public. At the 2012 ICCAT meeting in Morocco, the United States successfully maintained its annual limit of 250 recreationally caught blue and white marlin. Atlantic tunas remain a popular target of recreational fishermen. Approximately 25,000 Recreational and 4,000 Charter/Headboat permits were issued in 2012. The recreational fishery for Atlantic tunas remained open throughout the entire 2012 season. Private, charter, and headboat vessels had opportunities to catch fish of various size classes, especially in the highly regulated Atlantic Bluefin tuna fishery. Atlantic sharks remain a popular target for many recreational fishermen and the fishery remains viable whether it is for sharks that are allowed to be retained or catch and release fisheries. A proposed rule for Amendment 5 to the 2006 Consolidated Atlantic HMS Fishery Management Plan was published in December 2012 that includes proposed changes for the recreational shark fishery. More information about Amendment 5 may be found at http://www.nmfs.noaa.gov/sfa/hms/index.htm.
Improve Recreational Catch, Effort, and Status Data	Support the operation of Atlantic HMS tournaments and provide opportunities to obtain recreational catch and biological data on a variety of HMS species.	Implement the Recreational Bluefin Landings Tag (RBLT) Massachusetts Pilot Project.	Reviewing data collected during the 2012 pilot study, recovering unused tags for verification purposes, analysis and program evaluation currently underway, and will produce a final report with recommendations – expected early 2013.
Improve Recreational	Facilitate quick reporting of catch	Invest in the reporting	Data from tournament and non-tournament landings reports and other information are

Goal	Objective	Project(S)	Results
Catch, Effort, and Status Data	information by anglers through internet and phone reporting.	infrastructure for tournaments and individuals targeting billfish, and continues to investigate mechanisms that improve the timeliness of landings reports.	available in the 2012 Atlantic HMS Stock Assessment and Fishery Evaluation Report.
		Promote Live-release of shortfin mako and collect data from the public on catch and release location through shortfin mako web page and Android application of live-release maps.	To date, almost 200 active installs of the application have been conducted through which 13 releases have been reported. The shortfin mako release webpage is prominently displayed from the HMS home page.
Improve Recreational Catch, Effort, and Status Data	Improve timeliness of estimated landings from the Large Pelagic Survey (LPS) which will improve the availability of information for fishery management.	Develop and test Large Pelagic Survey improvements.	NOAA Science and Technology has initiated the process for the LPS program review and will explore updates similar to previous MRIP efforts.
	Support stock assessments of HMS species to provide a better picture of stock health and improve management of the fishery for recreational and commercial uses.	Collaborate with states, Atlantic HMS Advisory Panel, stakeholders, and NOAA Fisheries staff to improve data collection in the recreational yellowfin tuna fishery.	Atlantic HMS Management Division and the Southeast Fishery Science Center have initiated a process for improving tournament and non-tournament data collection programs, especially as they related to catch statistics in the recreational yellowfin tuna fishery.
	Implementation of Marine Recreational Information Program (MRIP) HMS Actions and Priorities.	Test a billfish catch card pilot program and an HMS recreational phone survey in Puerto Rico. Finalize project results and reports for the	Completed the pilot program and a final report. Completed the pilot program and a final report.

Regional Update: Atlantic Highly Migratory Species (Continued)

Goal	Objective	Project(S)	Results
		HMS for-hire Survey- Florida Pilot Study.	
		Conduct Pilot Phase-1 of a Massachusetts Recreational Bluefin Tuna Landings Census.	Reviewing data collected during the 2012 pilot study, recovering unused tags for verification purposes, analysis and program evaluation currently underway, and will produce a final report with recommendations – expected early 2013.
		Test for non-response bias in the Large Pelagics Telephone Survey.	Project has begun and is expected to continue in 2013.
		Conduct for-hire electronic logbook studies in the Gulf of Mexico.	Completed the projects and a report.
Improve Communications	Increase constituent awareness and understanding of Agency actions.	Implement and update the Atlantic HMS Recreational Fishing Action Agenda in cooperation with key stakeholders.	Provided NMFS with input to begin the process of updating the HMS Recreational Action Agenda following the HMS Advisory Panel during the Fall 2012 meeting. A dedicated discussion is scheduled for the May 2013 HMS Advisory Panel.
		Include recreational information on the HMS website.	In addition to having species specific links on the HMS home page that include recreational, as well as commercial, information, the HMS Management Division has included Careful Catch and Release, Compliance Guides, and non-tournament landings reporting links.
		Regularly update and distribute HMS News, Recreational compliance guide, Bluefin tuna guide, and shark identification placard for recreational stakeholders.	HMS News is updated and distributed each time the division takes an action or release a notice. The compliance guides that pertain to recreational and charter/ headboat fishing for HMS are updated annually and are readily available from the HMS website as well as in hard copy. Species identification guides are updated as needed and are readily available from the HMS species links from the HMS home page.
Improve Communications	Conduct on-the-ground communication efforts with constituents.	The collection of shortfin mako release data is underway via online and Android applications.	To date, almost 200 active installs of the application have been conducted through which 13 releases have been reported.
		Conduct outreach at boating, recreational, and species-specific	HMS staff regularly participates in various events that actively engage the recreational public at large. For example, New England

Goal	Objective	Project(S)	Results
		events.	Saltwater Fishing Show or the Massachusetts Striped Bass Association Annual Sport fishing Show to name a few. These opportunities are capitalized on when timing and funding allow.
		Identify constituents and constituent groups through Atlantic HMS tournament registration for distribution of outreach materials; facilitate biological data collection on landed HMS; and provide on-the-ground outreach to anglers.	This project is conducted annually. Tournament registration and other information may be found at http://www.nmfs.noaa.gov/sfa/hms/Tournaments/index.htm.
	Communicate information regarding major NOAA initiatives with constituents. Tournaments, and various associations that represent fishermen.	Collaborative outreach.	Information about major NOAA initiative is distributed through Atlantic HMS News (an e-mail news notice). Sign up for HMS News at http://www.nmfs.noaa.gov/sfa/hms/index.htm.
	Explore the feasibility of updating the benchmark analyses used to analyze socio-economic impacts of rules on recreational and commercial fishing communities.	Identify funding opportunities for benchmark socio-economic analyses.	NMFS strives to identify and facilitate funding through various sources.
Improve Social and Economic Data on Recreational Fisheries	Balanced recreational and commercial representation on the Atlantic HMS Advisory Panel.	Ensure balanced constituent representation.	Under the Magnuson-Stevens Act the HMS Advisory Panel must be balanced in its representation of commercial, recreational, and other interests. This is accomplished by having dedicated seats on the panel reserved for the various representation types. As individual terms expire they are filled from that same representation group.
Institutional Orientation	Improve institutional awareness.	Annual In-house planning sessions by the HMS recreational action	The HMS recreational action agenda coordination team is constantly interacting with from the HMS Management Division

Regional Update: Atlantic Highly Migratory Species (Continued)

Goal	Objective	Project(S)	Results
		agenda coordination team. This will include soliciting feedback from HMS leadership and HMS team members who interact regularly with constituents.	both through standing weekly divisional calls as well as more focused issue specific meetings.
		Briefing and discussion on the Atlantic HMS Recreational Action Agenda and activities with the Atlantic HMS AP during public meetings, as appropriate.	Agenda items with the HMS Advisory Panel during the Fall 2012 meeting provided NMFS with input to begin the process of updating the HMS Recreational Action Agenda. A dedicated discussion is also scheduled for the May 2013 HMS Advisory Panel. In addition, specific recreational issues/items are discussed in specific public meetings.
		Atlantic HMS Regional coordinators will coordinate with leadership within NMFS Office of Sustainable Fisheries to evaluate Atlantic HMS Action agenda on an annual basis. This includes regular meetings with the MAFAC working group for feedback.	Atlantic HMS Recreational Coordinators attended NMFS annual recreational coordinators meeting in Saint Petersburg, FL to discuss national and regional recreational fisheries initiatives.

REGIONAL UPDATE: SOUTHWEST

Goal	Objective	Project(S)	Results
Improve Recreational Fishing Opportunities	Participate in fishing events with a broad spectrum of stakehold-ers to improve steward-ship and adoption of ethical recreational fishing practices.	Ethical Angler Program participation at fishing events.	Participated in over ten fishing events on board Commercial Passenger Fishing Vessels (CPFV(s)) and at piers with youth, families, and veterans.
	Conduct research	Conduct Thresher	NMFS and the Pfleger Institute of

Goal	Objective	Project(S)	Results
	on best fishing practices to reduce post-release mortality in an effort to facilitate more sustainable fishing opportunities through higher survivorship of released fish.	Shark Post-release Mortality Study. Promote methods to reduce rockfish barotrauma mortality.	Environmental Research (PIER) were featured in an episode of the World Fishing Network's (WFN) IGFA Saltwater Adventures with Bill Boyce showcasing thresher shark research. Participated in the Pacific FishSmart Workshop in Portland, OR, May 8–9, 2012. The Sportfishing Association of California and the Golden Gate Fisherman's Association have provided fish descending devices to their member vessels.
Improve Recreational Catch, Effort, and Status Data	Improve recreational fisheries monitoring data for use in management.	Support the California Recreational Fisheries Survey.	Completed a relational database for Oregon's historical on-board Commercial passenger for hire vessel observer data. Development of the historical database for California's CPFV observer data is underway, with a current focus on error checking and database design.
	Conduct research on methods for reducing depredation and marine mammal interactions with anglers.	Research and Test Sea Lion Depredation Methods.	Created a one page flyer on pinniped deterrence for anglers.
	Conduct cooperative research projects with local anglers to improve understanding of recreational fishery effects and the importance of data collection, and monitoring.	Encourage HMS Biological Sample Donation. Encourage and support sighting reports – basking sharks. Continue rockfish surveys. Encourage and support HMS billfish tagging.	Collected stomachs, fin clips, otoliths, gonads or other organs, with help from over 50 individual anglers, from: 75 albacore, 381 bluefin tuna, 199 yellowfin tuna, 159 yellowtail, and 50 rockfish. Received reports of 78 basking shark sightings since 2011. Continued rockfish surveys. The billfish tagging program sent out about 2,200 billfish newsletters and received 487 billfish survey responses representing 416 tags for 2010, and 873 tags for 2011.
Improve Social and Economic Data on Recreational Fisheries	Conduct socio-economic research to determine how recreational fishing activities contribute to the California economy and jobs.	Conduct 2011 Angler Expenditure Survey.	The 2011 Angler Expenditure Survey data collection is complete and analysis is underway.
	Conduct socio-economic research and develop tools that can better inform management	Develop Decision-Making model of CPFV Operators and Anglers.	Research is underway for development of decision making models for CPFV operators and anglers.

Regional Update: Southwest (Continued)

Goal	Objective	Project(S)	Results
	decisions and other factors affecting the recreational fishing sector.		
Improve Social and Economic Data on Recreational Fisheries	Conduct socio-economic research and develop tools that can better inform management decisions and other factors affecting the recreational fishing sector.	Conduct assessment of dam removal on salmon and steelhead in Klamath River. Develop Valuation Model: Ocean Salmon Recreational Fisheries. Develop Valuation Model: In-River Salmon and Steelhead.	Wrote technical reports on economic effects of Klamath River dam removal on saltwater and in river recreational salmonid fishing. Developed a valuation model for the ocean recreational salmon fishery in California and Oregon, currently expanding the model to include groundfish. Postponed.
Improve Communication	Engage with sportfishing and outdoor media to improve communications on recreational fisheries issues; discuss issues with and provide information to constituents.	Participate in sportfishing radio shows and print media. Develop and Distribute Fact Sheets.	Several articles throughout the year featuring NMFS research in Western Outdoor News, and Pacific Coast Sportfishing. Developed and distributed basking shark and thresher shark fact sheets.
	Engage with stakeholders to hear concerns, share information, and collaborate on efforts, as appropriate.	Engage with Recreational Fishing Advisory Bodies. Attend Recreational Fishing Focused Conventions. Demonstrate / Present Ethical Angling and Best Fishing Practices.	Presented on the Southwest Action Agenda to the Channel Islands Sanctuary Advisory Committee. Staffed NMFS booths at two Fred Hall fishing shows and San Diego Day at theDocks. Presented on NMFS activities to several fishing clubs in southern, central, and northern California.
	Develop and maintain an informative website on recreational fisheries with current	Enhance Current Recreational Fishing Websites – SWRO, SWFSC.	Postponed.

Goal	Objective	Project(S)	Results
	information and tools to inform and assist anglers about management, stewardship practices, and opportunities.		
Institutional Orientation	Demonstrate Agency commitment to collaborating with recreational fishing constituents on strategies for improved management, stewardship, and research.	Meet with constituents annually to discuss issues and opportunities. Acknowledge constituents for exemplary Ethical Angling and Marine Resource Stewardship practices.	Held several listening sessions to obtain feedback from constituents on the Action Agenda. Postponed.
	Ensure that recreational fisheries issues are communicated and considered in research and management decisions.	Maintain effective internal communications.	Reporting regularly to the Regional Management Team on recreational fishing activities and increased awareness of recreational fishing issues in management decisions.

REGIONAL UPDATE: NORTHWEST

Goal	Objective	Project(S)	Results
Improve Recreational Fishing Opportunities	Consider means to incorporate barotrauma reduction devices into groundfish management.	Participate in FishSmart.	FishSmart led to an improved understanding of the engineering and performance of barotrauma reduction devices as well as the potential for their use by managers. On the West Coast, specific attention was paid to using barotrauma reduction devices to provide additional recreational opportunities in the context of overfished rockfish species.
	Incorporate barotrauma reduction devices into groundfish management.	PFMC groundfish management process.	PFMC is developing management alternatives for crediting recreational fishermen with reduced harvest rates when barotrauma reduction devices are utilized.

Regional Update: Northwest (Continued)

Goal	Objective	Project(S)	Results
	Develop and evaluate an abundance-based harvest management approach for ESA-listed Columbia River natural Tule fall Chinook Salmon.	A proposal, if found technically feasible, for an abundance-based harvest management approach to the Tule fall Chinook salmon for consideration by the Pacific Fishery Management Council and other co-managers.	Work on an abundance based harvest management plan for Tule Chinook salmon was completed in 2012 including review by the PFMC. NOAA Fisheries completed its ESA review of the plan and the plan was implemented for the first time in 2012.
	Establish and utilize the Snake Basin Harvest Forum to assist co-managers with reconciling fisheries to meet conservation and harvest objectives.	Reconciled tribal and recreational harvest plans in the Snake River and its tributaries for consideration and ESA determinations under Section 4(d).	NOAA Fisheries has worked with the Snake Basin Harvest Forum to complete review of state and tribal fisheries for spring/summer Chinook in the Salmon River Basin and northeast Oregon.
	Implement hatchery reform at programs funded through the Mitchell Act.	Provide funding for more than 20 salmon and steelhead hatchery facilities in the Columbia River through the Mitchell Act.	NOAA Fisheries has continued to provide funding for 20 Mitchell Act hatchery programs. Congress appropriated additional money in recent years to implement reforms. NF is working with the operators to prioritize and implement those reforms. NF is also scheduled to complete an EIS related to the Mitchell Act programs in 2013.
	Reduce pinniped and human conflicts in the Rogue River, OR.	Continue implementation of cooperative program in Gold Beach, OR.	In Gold Beach, Oregon, NMFS is a cooperator on a project to reduce nuisance pinnipeds from (1) taking angler-hooked fish, and (2) damaging Port of Gold Beach property (e.g., docks, marina). This project, in its seventh year of implementation, has been extremely effective in reducing conflict between humans and pinnipeds in the Rogue River estuary and marina. Local, state, and Federal government agencies, along with Gold Beach business leaders, pool their authorities, resources and expertise to humanely discourage seal and sea lion use of the estuary during a twelve

Goal	Objective	Project(S)	Results
			week period each summer/fall when the town of Gold Beach experiences a large influx of recreational boaters and fishers. Keeping the negative interaction between humans and pinnipeds to a minimum serves the agency's mission to recover, rebuild and sustain living marine resources, and to sustain coastal communities and economies.
Improve Recreational Catch, Effort, and Status Data	Explore cooperative research projects with recreational fishermen in Puget Sound.	Work with SeaDoc Society to identify cooperative research opportunities.	This work is ongoing. The expected results are for recreational fishermen and scientists to develop and participate in research projects on a collaborative basis.
	Conduct scientific workshops on the relationship of Chinook salmon harvest to Chinook abundance as prey for ESA-listed killer whales.	Co-host bi-lateral workshop to review the science relating to the effects of Chinook salmon fisheries to killer whales.	The workshop resulted in a better scientific understanding of the relationship between Chinook salmon harvest, including in recreational fisheries, to recovery of Southern Resident Killer Whales. A formal report by the Southern Resident Killer Whale Science Panel is expected in early Spring 2013.
Improve Recreational Catch, Effort, and Status Data	Review Lower Columbia River coho salmon harvest metric.	Host meetings among co-managers to discuss tasks and outline responsibilities for implementing the review.	Met with Oregon and Washington States to outline issues that would need to be addressed in a new LCR coho harvest matrix. The states are currently working on a new matrix that NOAA Fisheries is prepared to review once received.
Improve Social and Economic Data on Recreational Fisheries	Improve understanding of recreational constituent perspectives on rockfish recovery in Puget Sound.	Assess recreational fishing and rockfish recovery in Puget Sound using social science methods.	Published and made available to managers involved in ESA rockfish recovery efforts, "Angling for Insight: Examining the Recreational Fishing Community's Knowledge, Perceptions, Practices, and Preferences to Inform Rockfish Recovery Planning in Puget Sound, Washington" by J. Sawchuk. The report has improved managers understanding of varied perspectives on rockfish recovery in Puget Sound.
	Maintain and make available current estimations of economic effects	The Northwest Region will maintain, update, and publish a variety of	The Pacific Fishery Management Council publishes the Review of Ocean Salmon Fisheries every year that updates an extensive record of recreational salmon fishery data for the ocean and Puget Sound.

Regional Update: Northwest (Continued)

Goal	Objective	Project(S)	Results
	of recreational salmon fishing activities.	documents containing information about the economic value and effects of marine and freshwater recreational salmon fishing.	
Improve Communication	Conduct outreach to Northwest recreational fishing stakeholders.	Identify and coordinate with key recreational fishing stakeholders in the Northwest to target outreach.	NOAA Fisheries will be meeting with recreational fishery representatives on January 31 and the Seattle Boat Show to discuss issues of interest. The Boat Show has been used in recent years for annual meetings to maintain a close working relationship.
	Highlight Northwest activities in support of recreational fisheries.	Develop and distribute informational materials on Northwest activities in support of recreational fisheries.	New webpage to be launched in early 2013. Expected results are improved awareness and understanding of the NWR RecFish Initiative.
	Establish a constituent-led process for updating the NW Recreational Action Agenda.	Form Steering Committee with MAFAC RFWG and develop update strategy.	The representatives from the MAFAC RecFish Working Group are playing a leadership role in updating the NW Recreational Action Agenda.
Institutional Orientation	Reflect hatchery reforms in approved Hatchery Genetic Management Plans for the nearly 300 hatchery programs in the region. Improved internal awareness of recreational fisheries issues and priorities.	Approve HGMP and Resource Management Plans, with associated NEPA compliance. Internal Communications.	This work is ongoing. NOAA Fisheries has worked with the co-managers to identify and implement hatchery reforms through the HGMP consultation process. A number of these reviews have been completed, more are in process, and all are scheduled for completion over the next two years. The NWR staff has an ongoing focus on recreational fishery issues that arise through their review of harvest and hatchery related actions.

REGIONAL UPDATE: ALASKA

Goal	Objective	Project(S)	Results
Improve Recreational Fishing Opportunities	Ensure quality recreational fishing habitat.	Work on restoration projects for coastal, marine, and anadromous fish habitats.	NMFS conducted a foot survey to assess marine debris. As of August 2012, this survey has covered 220 km and has categorized Tsunami debris from Japan. In addition, NMFS continues work with fish habitat partners throughout the State of Alaska to restore coastal wetlands.
Improve Recreational Catch, Effort, and Status Data	Create reporting system for tracking halibut caught under the proposed Guided Angler Fish Program (GAF).	Create a web and phone based application to allow electronic reporting.	The project is ongoing due to a delay in implementation of the final rule for the guided angler catch sharing plan.
	Grant the State of Alaska funds to improve coded wire tag recovery for sport-caught Chinook salmon.	Increase port sampler presence to improve data collection of coded wire tags.	The port sampler presence has been increased by 8 staff, and a report by the State of Alaska about coded wire tag data collection is anticipated in 2013.
	Improve accessibility and quality of recreational catch and effort data reported in the sport charter logbook program.	Grant federal assistance to the State of Alaska to improve data access and quality control by using image recognition software.	The assistance has been provided to the state, which is now using image recognition software.
Improve Social and Economic Data on Recreational Fisheries	Economic and social survey.	Conduct a social survey about angler fishing behavior in Alaska.	The voluntary survey is currently in the field.
	Create an Alaska recreational charter vessel guide and owner data collection system.	Create data instruments for gathering cost and earnings information in the saltwater charter fishing vessel sector in Alaska.	The survey has been tested and being fielded.
Improve Communication	Create recreational fishing constituent database to help establish regular and better communication.	Develop recreational fishery list-serve and newsletter.	Anglers were encouraged to provide e-mail information at the Anchorage sport show and a signup portal was added the NMFS Alaska Region website.

Regional Update: Alaska (Continued)

Goal	Objective	Project(S)	Results
			An angler database was created and a newsletter sent out to constituents in 2012.
			This list will be used in the future for communication with constituents
	Create recreational-fishing themed booth and educational material to be on display.	Design a booth and educational materials and presented at a recreational fisheries events.	In partnership with the NOAA Office of Law Enforcement, outreach was conducted at the Anchorage Sport Show in March 2012.
	Develop a website hosted by NMFS Alaska Region that is designed specifically for recreational fishers.	Publish a user-friendly website designed to provide fishing information.	Major changes were made to the website in 2012 and further changes are planned for 2013.

REGIONAL UPDATE: PACIFIC ISLANDS

Goal	Objective	Project(S)	Results
Improve Recreational Fishing Opportunities	Reduce post-release mortality of recreationally-caught fish.	Barbless Circle Hook Project.	Successful and thorough outreach to promote and educate the public on the use of barbless circle hooks for recreational fishing; to improve condition and reduce post-release mortality of catch-and-released fish to increase their numbers to enhance recreational fishing opportunities for the future.
	Maximize benefits of recreational tagging programs.	Tagging program coordination and collaboration.	Information gathering and compilation of tagging program details (species, tag type, tag legend, reward, contact #s, etc.) for dissemination to public to increase recapture reporting rates. Promotion of materials and methods to minimize stress and maximize post-release survival. Promotion of data analyses for information useful for sustainable management.
	Improve FAD programs and efficiency.	Workshop to investigate FAD issues.	Organized a PI regional meeting on FADs with an emphasis on minimizing costs, evaluating advances in mooring

Goal	Objective	Project(S)	Results
			systems and FAD design and maximizing deployment times and aggregation efficiency. Scheduled February 13–14, 2013.
	Prevent overfishing on recreational fish stocks.	Protect recreational fish stocks by instituting Annual Catch Limits/Accountability Measures to prevent overfishing.	Annual catch limits and Accountability Measures are in place for all federally managed stocks.
Improve Recreational Catch, Effort, and Status Data	Improve collection of non-commercial fishery data.	A memorandum of understanding on the exchange of confidential fisheries information between Hawaii State and NOAA Fisheries.	Completed, and being used for data exchange
		Collaborate with/support the State in modifying its Vessel Registration System, Division of Boating and Ocean Recreation (DBOR), to serve as a vehicle for fisheries data collection.	Executed a grant to the Hawaii DBOR for the modification of vessel registration forms and database, established public online registration access at boat harbor offices, and improved the online vessel registration system to allow differentiation of vessels used for recreational fishing. Ongoing. The vessel registration database will be used in future boat-based catch and effort sampling to support a proposed Hawaii regional survey. The regional survey will support a Hawaii request for exemption to the National Saltwater Angler Registry Program.
		Improve collection of catch information from Hawaii for-hire sector.	Developing an outreach brochure to notify/remind for-hire vessel owners and operators of existing State and Federal requirements for charter fishing vessels, including requirement to obtain State licenses and submit fishing reports.
		Improve data quality and ability to utilize data collected by the Hawaii Marine Recreational Fishing Survey (HMRFS).	Project reviewed existing HMRFS program to evaluate possible improvements. MRIP consultants provided a review and recommendations to the program and a HMRFS review was conducted July 16–19, 2012 that provided the State with a set of recommendations.

Regional Update: Pacific Islands (Continued)

Goal	Objective	Project(S)	Results
	Understand the universe of non-commercial fishermen in federal waters and select trip attributes.	Mail Survey of Hawaii's Registered Boaters.	A working group of managers, scientists, and fishermen developed the survey instrument and protocol in 2012. The survey will be fielded in 2013.
Improve Social and Economic Data on Recreational Fisheries	Collect information about the main issues impacting recreational and subsistence fishermen in American Samoa and Guam.	American Samoa and Guam Fishing Community Profile Updates.	Interviews were conducted and these data will be included in the upcoming American Samoa Fishing Community Profile Update Administrative Report and the Guam Fishing Community Profile Update Administrative Report.
	Collect information about fishermen's (and other stakeholders') perceptions regarding the condition of coral reef resources, threats to those resources, and the extent to which they would support various management efforts.	Survey of Hawaii Resident Resource Users' Knowledge, Attitudes and Perceptions of Coral Reefs in Two Hawaii Priority Sites.	Surveys are currently being conducted in South Kohala on the Big Island, and will begin this spring/summer in Kahekili on Maui.
	Document past and contemporary trips to the Islands Unit of the Marianas Trench Marine National Monument and collect data regarding the historical and cultural connections of CNMI and Guam residents to the islands and waters of the Islands Unit.	Documenting Traditional Fishing in the Islands Unit of the Marianas Trench Marine National Monument.	Interviews completed, outreach brochure published, and final report being compiled (Jan 2013).
	Describe	CNMI and Hawaii	Final drafts of these reports are being

Goal	Objective	Project(S)	Results
	recreational, sport, and subsistence fishing in Hawaii and CNMI, and document the islands' connection to and dependence on fishing.	Fishing Community Profiles.	edited and will be published soon.
	Collection of accurate and comprehensive information on the value of marine recreational fisheries.	2011 National Marine Recreational Fishing Expenditure Survey.	Results of the National Marine Recreational Fishing expenditure survey are being finalized. A brochure of Hawaii results has been designed and will be printed and distributed once regional impact assessments are published by NOAA headquarters.
	Obtain improved economic information on charter fishing fleet.	2012 Hawaii Charter Cost-Earnings Survey.	Undertook a 2012 Hawaii Charter Cost-Earnings Survey.
	Increase understanding of the social importance of fishing to Hawaiian communities that can also be used as a model for conducting similar research throughout the region.	Conduct a study to Understand the flow of non-commercial catch in Hawaiian communities at University of Hawaii, Hilo.	Social science researcher contracted to conduct study on flow of non-commercial catch through small Hawaiian communities. Surveys and fieldwork are completed and a report will publish soon.
Improve Communication	Enable recreational fishermen from American Samoa, CNMI, Guam, and Hawaii to participate in NMFS activities in fisheries, habitat conservation, and protected species programs and to help develop recreational fisheries initiatives.	Hold a Pacific Islands regional recreational summit in 2012.	NOAA Fisheries hosted a three-day meeting of 28 invited fishery constituents from American Samoa, the Northern Mariana Islands, Guam and Hawaii, August 21–23, 2012, to help the agency identify recreational fishery projects for possible implementation in FY-2013. Highlights of the summit included a poster session, digital polling, roundtable discussions, and consensus-based format. The delegates concluded the summit by proposing via real-time electronic polling, 21 potential projects for consideration by NOAA Fisheries.
	Improve quality of online information and resources for recreational fishing	Re-development of recreational fisheries web content.	In 2012 the website was updated to include new links to weather, buoys, tides, state and federal fishing regulations, and more. Content for

Regional Update: Pacific Islands (Continued)

Goal	Objective	Project(S)	Results
	in the Pacific Islands Region.		recreational fishing statistics for the Pacific Islands Region, surveys, and National Angler Registry was also updated. Ongoing.
	Improve recreational fisheries outreach and education.	Develop useful outreach materials that discuss the importance of recreational fisheries.	Created an educational brochure that highlighted the importance of fishing in Hawaii, information on the top pelagic species caught in Hawaii, and local recipes for fish. Distributed widely to charterboat operators in the region.
	Engage public on the value and importance of recreational fishing in the Pacific Islands Region.	Participate in local fishing related events.	Developed fishing-related games and materials for children and families to engage in during fishing and ocean-related events, for example. The Hawaiian Fishing and Seafood Festival, October 7, 2012.
	Improving information flow and dialogue with recreational fishing associations, clubs and the fishing public.	Public outreach on recreational fishing issues.	Recreational Fisheries Specialist provided presentations and Q&A sessions to fishing clubs and to the fishing constituency at public meetings held in conjunction with Fishery Council meetings.
	Foster communication with the recreational fishing community.	Promoting outreach and contact with the recreational fishing sector.	Created a publicly accessible email address where the public can submit any and all concerns regarding recreational/non-commercial fisheries (PIRO.Recfish@noaa.gov). Published articles on recreational fishery issues for the Pacific Islands Region in fishing magazines and periodicals.
Institutional Orientation	Strengthen and then maintain NOAA Fisheries' ability to manage for the goals of Pacific Islands recreational/non-commercial fisheries.	Hire a Marine Recreational Fisheries Specialist.	Fishery Management Specialist (Recreational) recruited to NOAA Fisheries, Pacific Islands Regional Office (September 24, 2012).
	Establish dialogue and foster collaboration between the Marine Recreational Fisheries Specialist and regional	Internal outreach and collaboration.	Meet with and update PIR and Science Center programs/personnel on the goals and objectives of the recreational fisheries program within PIR/SFD and seek areas for collaboration and mutual benefit.

Goal	Objective	Project(S)	Results
	personnel.		
	Establish dialogue and foster collaboration between the Marine Recreational Fisheries Specialist and other NOAA entities.	External NOAA/PIR outreach and collaboration.	Meet with and update Fishery Council staff, Council advisory groups/committees, Council members and MAFAC Recreational Fisheries Working Group members on the goals and objectives of the recreational fisheries program within PIR/SFD and seek areas for collaboration and mutual benefit.
	Establish dialogue and foster collaboration between the Marine Recreational Fisheries Specialist and fisheries related research and educational institutions.	External outreach and collaboration.	Meet with and update representatives of fishery research programs, universities and fishery researchers on the goals and objectives of the recreational fisheries program within PIR/SFD and seek areas for collaboration and mutual benefit.
	Establish dialogue and foster collaboration between the Marine Recreational Fisheries Specialist and the recreational fishing constituency.	External outreach and collaboration.	Communicate with fishermen and representatives of all recreational fishing sectors through specific meetings, conference calls, fishing club meetings and workshops. Provide presentations to the public on issues impacting and important to recreational fisheries.

In: Recreational Fisheries in the U.S.
Editor: Ellen K. Parker

ISBN: 978-1-63485-595-2
© 2016 Nova Science Publishers, Inc.

Chapter 4

THE ECONOMICS OF THE RECREATIONAL FOR-HIRE FISHING INDUSTRY IN THE NORTHEAST UNITED STATES 2ND EDITION[*]

Scott Steinback and Ayeisha Brinson

EXECUTIVE SUMMARY

Nearly 1.6 million passengers fished aboard for-hire recreational fishing vessels during 2011 in the Northeast United States (ME – NC). While the National Marine Fisheries Service (NMFS) regularly collects detailed catch, effort, and expenditure information from anglers fishing aboard for-hire vessels, no data are collected about the business structure and costs of the marine for-hire fishing industry operating in the Northeast. This study is intended to fill that gap.

Voluntary mail, telephone, and in-person surveys were designed to collect information on annual costs, returns, business structure, effort, demographics, and attitudinal data from for-hire vessel owners in the Northeast from January 2011 through July 2011. Surveys were completed by 295 vessel owners who provided data on 332 distinct for-hire vessels in the Northeast.

Survey results show that the overall financial condition of marine recreational for-hire fishing businesses in the Northeast is mixed. Assets

---

[*] This is an edited, reformatted and augmented version of a publication, Northeast Fisheries Science Center Reference Document 13-03, issued by the National Oceanic and Atmospheric Administration, April 2013.

exceed liabilities by over four times for the average charter and head boat, and over 90% of charter and head boat owners carry insurance coverage. This implies that a rather strong financial for-hire fishing fleet exists in the Northeast. The results also reveal that the average charter boat produced only a little over $5.1 thousand in net income in 2010 and that over half of the charter boats in the Northeast actually incurred higher expenses than revenues in 2010. In contrast, the average head boat generated over $95.1 thousand in net income in 2010 although median net income per head boat was lower at $50.1 thousand.

In addition to providing a detailed overview of the operating structure of the "average" Northeast for-hire head boat and charter boat, we constructed an input-output model to estimate the economic activity that for-hire businesses contribute to the Northeast's economy as measured by total employment, labor income, and sales. Model results show that in 2010 the for-hire industry earned $140.3 million in revenue, generated $50.4 million in income to owners, hired captains, crew/mates, and office staff, and employed over 6,200 individuals. The multiplier effects of this activity were substantial. An additional $193.7 million in sales, $66.5 million in income, and 1,290 jobs in other businesses in the Northeast were supported by the for-hire industry through indirect and induced transactions. Service businesses (real estate, food services, marinas, repair shops, etc.), wholesale and retail trade businesses (sporting goods stores, bait shops, gas stations, etc.), and manufacturing businesses (fishing gear manufactures, fuel refineries, commercial fishermen [bait], etc.) were the enterprises most reliant on the for-hire fleet. Over 700 service sector jobs, 360 wholesale and retail trade jobs, and 63 manufacturing jobs were dependent upon the for-hire fleet in the Northeast in 2010. In total, an estimated 7,530 jobs, in the overall Northeast regional economy, were supported by the active for-hire fleet in 2010.

1. INTRODUCTION

The for-hire recreational fishing industry along the northeastern coast of the United States (ME – NC), provides an important outdoor leisure service for many individuals and sustains economic activity in the form of sales, income, and employment throughout the region. In 2011, nearly 1.6 million passengers fished aboard for-hire boats operating in marine waters of the Northeast.[1] While the National Marine Fisheries Service (NMFS) regularly collects detailed catch, effort, and expenditure information from anglers fishing aboard for-hire vessels, no data are collected about the business structure and costs of the marine for-hire fishing industry operating in the

Northeast. This study is intended to fill that gap. In addition to providing a detailed overview of the operating structure of the "average" Northeast for-hire head boat and charter boat, we estimate the economic activity that for-hire businesses contribute to the Northeast's economy as measured by total employment, labor income, and sales.

1.1. Motivation/Purpose

Comprehensive economic data on the Northeast's for-hire industry are currently unavailable. We located only two published studies in the last ten years that examined the operating side of the for-hire recreational fishing industry in the Northeast. Dumas et al. (2009) provided detailed economic data on the charter and head boat fleet, but their study was limited to for-hire boats operating only out of North Carolina - the southernmost state included in our study. Holland et al. (2012) also examined the economics of for-hire businesses in North Carolina. As their study also concentrated on for-hire businesses operating in southeastern states, their findings and the findings of Dumas et al. (2009) are not likely to be representative of the entire for-hire industry operating in the Northeast.

The lack of data concerning for-hire operations in the Northeast makes it difficult to determine the importance of the for-hire industry to the Northeast's economy and to adequately address how proposed management actions might affect business operations. Numerous legislative mandates (e.g., Magnuson-Stevens Act, Regulatory Flexibility Act, National Environmental Policy Act, Executive Order 12866 and others) require that the NMFS assess the economic impacts of proposed fisheries policies. Typically, the focus of such assessments is on likely changes in angler behavior, not on how proposed policies will impact for-hire business operations. Although these assessments may contain estimates of how overall gross revenues for the for-hire fleet will be affected, widespread assumptions are generally required to derive these estimates, including the notion that operating costs remain constant. The data collected in this study provide information to alleviate these problems.

The primary goals of the study are to:

1) Provide a comprehensive overview of the economic condition of the for-hire industry in the Northeast;
2) Estimate the contribution of the for-hire industry to the overall economy in the Northeast; and,

3) Collect the data necessary for the development of economic models used to assess how for-hire businesses operations are affected by proposed management policies.

2. METHODOLOGY

A voluntary in-person survey was designed to collect information on annual costs, returns, business structure, effort, demographics, and attitudinal data from for-hire vessel owners. NMFS contracted with QuanTech Inc., a survey research firm with recreational for-hire fishery data collection expertise, and Gentner Consulting Group (GCG), a natural resources economics and public opinion research company, to conduct the Recreational For-Hire Economic Survey (RFHES) from January 2011 through July 2011.

Outreach / Pretests

A press release about the study was prepared and forwarded to for-hire organizations in the Northeast during fall 2010 (see Table 1 for list of organizations). Many organizations published the press release on their websites or emailed it to their members. In addition, GCG attended board meetings hosted by the Rhode Island Party and Charter Association (RIPCA) and the Northeast Charter Boat Captains Association (NCBCA), to provide information about the study and to obtain feedback on draft survey instruments.

During outreach calls to the for-hire associations, board members were asked if they would be willing to have their members participate in the design process. All but three organizations were eager to assist and supplied comments on draft survey instruments via email and telephone. GCG also conducted 15 in-depth interviews with for-hire owners who owned 21 vessels. Substantial feedback was obtained during this synergistic pretesting approach, which significantly improved the final survey instrument. For example, during the pretests, it was apparent that respondents had a difficult time answering trip-level financial questions. If trip level cost information was collected and then aggregated to estimate annual financial information, there was the potential for major digit bias. Therefore, based upon this feedback, the survey was revised and only annual financial information was collected.

2.1. Population and Sampling Frame

The RFHES sampling frame was a subset of the Wave 1 2011 For-Hire Telephone Survey (FHTS) vessel directory maintained by NMFS for the Marine Recreational Information Program (MRIP).[2] The FHTS vessel directory is a comprehensive list of for-hire vessels on the U.S. Atlantic coast from Georgia through Maine. The FHTS is updated on a regular basis and distinguishes vessels by vessel type (charter boat/head boat) and geographic area. The FHTS distinguishes charter boats from head boats by the carrying capacity of passengers. Charter boats are defined as boats that are licensed by the Coast Guard to carry up to six passengers and head boats are licensed by the U.S. Coast Guard to carry more than six passengers.

The RFHES sampling frame included charter and head boat vessels with a primary port located in the Northeast (NC, VA, MD, DE, NJ, NY, CT, RI, MA, NH, or ME); however, there were some exclusions. Only vessels with a valid address were included in the sampling frame because the survey methodology utilized a prenotification postcard. This did not disqualify many vessels since almost all of the vessels in the vessel directory had a valid mailing address (only 13 vessels lacked a mailing address in the areas sampled by the RFHES). Second, the vessel directory includes some vessels with Highly Migratory Species (HMS) charter boat/head boat permits that do not charter. These vessels were excluded from the RFHES and were identified by information in the comments field such as "HAS HMS CH/HB PERMIT BUT DOES NOT CHARTER." Third, vessels that were contacted by a North Carolina economic survey in 2010 (for Holland et al. 2012) were not included in the RFHES sampling frame. Finally, duplicate vessels were removed from the RFHES sampling frame. Duplicate vessels exist in the FHTS vessel directory because some vessels operate in more than one state. Some vessel owners move their for-hire business south in the winter to keep their operations running year round. Contact information may be different on the two duplicated vessel records; therefore, instead of just removing duplicates at random, the duplicated record assigned to a state further north was removed from the RFHES sampling frame.

All head boats contained in the Wave 1 FHTS directory frame were selected for the survey. A sample of charter boats was selected by using simple random sampling from the amended RFHES sampling frame. After the sample was drawn, addresses from the vessel records without telephone numbers were sent to a White Pages reverse address search service (http://pro.whitepages.com/). A total of 1,676 vessels with telephone numbers and addresses were selected (1,506 charter boats and 170 head boats) for the RFHES. This represented 42% of the charter boats contained in the amended Wave 1 RFHES sampling frame and 100% of the head boats. The resulting distributions of randomly selected vessels by state and vessel type are shown in Table 2.

2.2. Implementation

QuanTech mailed presurvey notification packages to owners/representatives of the vessels randomly selected from the RFHES sampling frame. The notification package included a cover letter describing the survey (Appendix I), a list of frequently asked questions (FAQs) with answers about the survey (Appendix II), a copy of the survey questionnaire (Appendix III), and a small token of appreciation (a new $5 bill), to encourage participation. The packages were mailed in six "waves." In each wave, packages were mailed to potential respondents located in one or more states as follows:

- Wave 1: MD, DE, and Phase 1 VA – 249 packages mailed January 12, 2011;
- Wave 2: NC and Phase 2 VA – 235 packages mailed January 26, 2011;
- Wave 3: NJ and PA – 282 packages mailed February 9, 2011;
- Wave 4: NY, CT, and RI – 332 packages mailed February 23, 2011;
- Wave 5: MA Phase 1– 297 packages mailed March 9, 2011; and
- Wave 6: MA Phase 2, NH, and ME – 217 packages mailed March 23, 2011.

Approximately 7-10 days after the packages were mailed, trained QuanTech telephone interviewers called the vessel owners/representatives to follow up on the package and screen for eligibility.[3] Vessel owners were eligible to be surveyed if they were active in 2010 (i.e., took passengers fishing for a fee in 2010) and if no more than 50% of their trips targeted HMS.[4]

The screening calls were also used to encourage survey participation by the owners and to answer any questions they might have prior to scheduling an in-person interview. When an eligible owner agreed to participate, the screening interviewer provided the vessel owner with the name of the person who would be contacting them to schedule a personal interview. Screening data were collected during the recruitment calls whereas RFHES cost and earnings data were collected during the in-person interviews.

Table 3 shows the results of RFHES screening calls. QuanTech called the 1,676 vessel records with a telephone number to completion. That is, owners of 1,676 vessels agreed to participate in the survey, refused to participate in the study, were ineligible for the survey, did not own the vessel (or any other for-hire vessel nor could they provide contact information for the current owner), or were called 10 times without being contacted, or the phone number was bad (disconnected) or incorrect. Many vessel records required additional call attempts or in some cases, QuanTech reached someone but was told to call back. Additional call attempts were made when asked to call back. The percent of respondents that QuanTech attempted to contact who agreed to participate in the survey during the screening calls ranged from 12.5% in NH to 52% in ME. Refusals were highest in MD (25.7%) and DE (25.6%) and lowest in CT and ME (8.0%). Owners that could not be reached after 10 calls and owners that were ineligible to participate accounted for approximately 54% of the total screening calls. The most common reason for ineligibility was that the vessel was inactive during all of 2010 (79% of ineligibles). Approximately 2% of the owners QuanTech attempted to contact indicated that they no longer owned the for-hire vessel, and about 8% of the owners could not be reached because the telephone number was incorrect.

During the initial calls to for-hire owners to screen for eligibility to participate in the RFHES in-person survey, it became evident that, although the RFHES was designed as an in-person survey, some respondents indicated a preference to participate by mail, email, or telephone. To maximize the potential pool of respondents, the data collection procedure was modified to accommodate a respondent's preferred method for participating in the survey. QuanTech used a CAPI (Computer Assisted Personal Interviewing) system to capture electronic data in the field. When necessary, data were captured on the phone with the same system operated as a CATI (Computer Assisted Telephone Interviewing) system. Data from mailed or emailed responses, which usually required a telephone follow-up, were entered into the CAPI system by office staff.

Following a procedure modified from Dillman (2000), QuanTech sent follow-up letters explaining the importance of participating in the survey, including a stamped return envelope and a copy of the questionnaire. Follow-up mailings were sent to those who indicated that they would participate by mail but had not returned a completed questionnaire and to those who agreed to participate in person but subsequently could not be contacted to schedule an interview. A second follow-up letter was sent one month later to vessel owners who had recently indicated that they would mail-in their survey. A final round of follow-up packages was sent six weeks later by priority mail to those who had not responded and whose packages had not been returned undeliverable. The final follow-up package contained a copy of the questionnaire and a letter explaining that the survey was drawing to a close so time to participate was running out.

QuanTech finished RFHES data collection efforts on July 31, 2011. Table 4 shows the RFHES final survey results for the vessel owners that were contacted. Of the 367 vessel owners who agreed to participate in the survey during screening, 38% (141) participated in person, 7% (24) participated by phone, 35% (130) participated by mail/email, and 20% (72) never completed the survey.

The 295 vessel owners with whom interviews were conducted provided data on 332 distinct for-hire vessels in the Northeast. Some vessel owners owned more than one vessel, and owners of multiple vessels were asked about all their vessels whenever one was selected from the RFHES.

2.3. Data Cleaning

Survey responses were tested in Statistical Analysis Software (SAS) for internal consistency. To maximize the useable responses, outliers and inconsistent observations were eliminated without removing the entire record.[5] Although it would have been preferable to use only data from respondents who completed every relevant survey question, the amount of data available did not allow for this more restrictive interpretation of a response. Thus, incomplete records were included in the financial assessments under the assumption that the sample responses reflect the true population parameters. Reasonable sample sizes exist for all reported results, so the sample responses are considered representative of the entire for-hire fleet in the Northeast. Additionally, missing income and cost values were converted to zero values when appropriate, and because of difficulty assigning financial data to a particular vessel, cost and earnings information from vessel owners who owned both charter and head boats were excluded from the financial analyses.

3. RESULTS

Our survey results are generally reported as arithmetic means (i.e., averages) for both the nonfinancial and financial data. Confidence intervals, standard deviations, and median values are provided for all of the financial data. Of the for-hire owners that were successfully contacted and eligible to complete the survey (615 owners), 295 completed the survey for an effective response rate of 48%. Overall, we were satisfied with the response rate, given the type of information being requested from for-hire owners (i.e., personal and financial information about their business activities). We report only region-wide values because of sample size constraints at the state level. In addition, the reader is reminded that there is variation in operations across head boats and charter boats in the Northeast so "average" values may not appropriately characterize every vessel in the fleet.

3.1. Vessel Characteristics

The average charter boat vessel in the Northeast was 30ft in length, with a 360 horsepower engine and could accommodate 9 passengers. Approximately 41% of respondents purchased "new" charter boats with a mean sale price of $80,000. The average charter boat was built 16 years ago and purchased about 8 years ago. Charter boat vessels employed (on average) 0.2 full-time crew members and 0.5 part-time crew members; that is, for approximately three months of the year an average charter boat may employ one full-time crew member and one part-time crew member for six months of the year. Most (88%) charter boats were made of fiberglass, and two-thirds of respondents docked or moored their vessels (Table 5).

The average head boat in the Northeast was 63 ft in length, with an 876 horsepower engine that accommodated about 91 passengers. The typical head boat vessel was built about 32 years ago; however, on average respondents purchased their head boats 14 years ago. One-third of head boat vessels were purchased new for a price of approximately $230,000. Head boat vessels employed approximately two full-time employees and one and one-half part-time employees. One-half of head boats were made of wood, while the other half were made of fiberglass (27%) and aluminum (18%;Table 5).

3.2. Vessel Operations

Nearly all (97%) of charter boat vessels were run by owner-operators. Two-thirds of charter boat businesses were established as sole proprietorships, while 21% were Limited Liability Corporations (LLCs) and 14% were corporations. Approximately two-thirds of head boat vessels were run by owner-operators. Twenty-four percent of head boat respondents were owners who employed either a corporate captain (9%) or a private captain (2%). In contrast to charter boats, three-quarters of head boat businesses were established as corporations, while 17% were Limited Liability Corporations (LLCs) and 5% were sole proprietorships (Table 6).

Many respondents took trips without patrons. For example, forty-six percent of charter boat respondents took trips without passengers to collect bait. On average, charter boat vessels took nine trips that lasted under three hours to catch bait in 2010. Approximately two-thirds of charter boat respondents took trips to scout new locations without any passengers. On average, these scouting trips lasted under five hours, and charter boat respondents took approximately ten per year in 2010. Approximately one-half of charter boat respondents took nonfishing trips for whale watching or sightseeing; respondents took fewer than five of these types of trips in 2010. Less than 10% of head boats took trips to catch bait and, on average, these vessels took eight trips that lasted less than three hours. One-third of head boats went on scouting trips that lasted under five hours and totaled about three trips in 2010. Sixty percent of head boats took nonfishing trips, such as whale watching or sightseeing, totaling about 24 trips in 2010 (Table 6).

3.3. Owner Characteristics

On average, charter boat and head boat owners were in their 50s. Head boat owners tended to have more experience as an owner or captain (25 years) than charter boat owners (14 years). Less than one-quarter of the total 2010 income of charter boat owners was earned from their for-hire activities, while the 2010 income of head boat owners' was predominately (70%) from for-hire activities (Table 7).

3.4. Fishing Trip Types

For-hire operations offered a variety of trip types to their patrons, including half-day, full-day, or overnight trips. Most (85%) charter boat owners offered half-day trips. In 2010, charter boat owners took on average 26 trips that lasted under five hours with approximately four passengers. On average, one of the half-day trips was a charitable donation. More than half (14 trips) of the half-day trips occurred in the summer months (July – September); about seven trips were taken in the spring (April – June). The fewest half-day trips occurred during October – March. About 14% of these trips were taken in federal fishing waters. On average, charter boat owners earned about $450 for each of these trips in 2010 (Table 8).

Two-thirds of head boat owners offered half-day trips in 2010. The average head boat took 203 half-day trips with approximately 27 passengers that lasted 4.4 hours. On average, fewer than three of these half-day trips were provided as a charitable donation. More than half of the half-day trips were in the summer and one-quarter occurred in the spring. Approximately 15% of the half-day trips were taken in federal fishing waters. On average, head boat owners charged $32 per person for each of these trips in 2010.

Nearly all charter (90%) and head boat (72%) owners offered full-day fishing trips. In 2010, each charter boat offered an average of 19 full-day trips and each head boat offered 69 full-day trips. Charter boat trips accommodated fewer than five passengers, while head boat trips had 21 passengers on average. Full-day trips lasted eight and one-half hours for charter boat or eight hours for head boat trips. The majority of the full day trips occurred in the summer for charter boat vessels (10 trips). For head boat vessels the peak season was longer, including the spring (28 trips) and summer (26 trips). The average fee for full-day trips was $700 for charter boat and $91 per person for head boat trips. About one-third of these full-day trips occurred in federal waters for both types of trips in the for-hire sector.

About thirteen percent of for-hire owners offered overnight trips. Charter boat owners took two overnight trips, on average, in 2010, while head boat owners took 11 trips. Most overnight trips occurred in the summer and lasted about 24 hours. Charter boat trips accommodated five anglers, on average, while head boat trips accommodated 19 passengers. The vast majority of the overnight trips were in federal waters for charter boats (63%) and head boats (100%). Charter boat owners charged on average $1,900 for overnight trips (all passengers), while head boat owners charged $290 per person.

One-quarter of for-hire owners offered nonfishing trips on their vessels. The purpose of these trips tended to be for sightseeing, whale watching, or bird watching. In 2010, charter boat owners took approximately 10 nonfishing trips, while head boat owners took 34 nonfishing trips. Nonfishing trips on charter boats accommodated five passengers and lasted 7.5 hours, on average. Nonfishing trips on head boats accommodated 32 passengers and lasted 9.5 hours. Charter boats spent 32% of these nonfishing trips in federal waters, while head boats spent 54% of these nonfishing trips in federal waters. On average, the fee charged to rent a charter boat was $520, and the per person fee to fish aboard a head boat was $73.

3.5. Cost and Earnings

3.5.1. Balance Sheet

Information on assets and liabilities of for-hire businesses was used to generate a balance sheet for the average for-hire vessel. A balance sheet provides a financial snapshot of a vessel's activity. The balance sheet approach used here compares average assets to liabilities and was modeled after Liese and Travis (2010) and Savolainen et al. (2012). Assets are measured as the market value of the vessel at the end of 2010, whereas liabilities include the investment required to acquire those assets, and are calculated from the value of outstanding vessel and operating loans. Owner's equity is the difference between assets and liabilities.

In 2010, the average charter boat vessel's equity was $48.4 thousand (Table 9). Average assets were $65.0 thousand, the average outstanding vessel loan was $16.0 thousand, and the average outstanding short-term operating loan was $762. The average market value of the vessel (asset value) was approximately $9.0 thousand lower than the average vessel purchase price of $74.3 thousand. Thirty percent of charter boat owners had outstanding vessel loans and only six percent had short-term operating loans.

In 2010, the average head boat owner's equity was $160.8 thousand (Table 10). Average assets were $241.8 thousand, the average outstanding vessel loan was $59.4 thousand, and the average outstanding short-term operating loan was $3.6 thousand. The average asset value (market value) was approximately $24.1 thousand lower than the vessel purchase price of $265.9 thousand. Forty-five percent of head boat owners had outstanding vessel loans, and approximately 20% had short-term operating loans.

3.5.2. Cash Flow

In contrast to a balance sheet, cash flow is a financial statement of a vessel owner's flow of money over time. In this case, the cash flow is the revenue generated through charter or head boat trips. Inflows are the revenues accruing to a vessel owner through trip sales. Outflows or expenditures represent the costs of owning and operating a for-hire vessel. Outflows in the for-hire industry include the costs of fuel and oil, bait, ice, food and drink, tackle and supplies, vessel repair and maintenance, insurance, overhead, costs for captain and crew, investment payments, and loan payments (Table 11). The difference between inflows and outflows represents an owner's liquidity or solvency and is described as net cash flow. Net cash flow is a measure of short-term viability for a vessel owner (Liese and Travis 2010). Appendix IV contains a statistical summary of the individual survey questions used in the cash flow statements.

In 2010, the average charter boat owner's net cash flow was $5.2 thousand (Table 12).[6] Inflows totaled $27.7 thousand for an average vessel. The largest expenditure for the average charter boat vessel was for overhead ($4.9 thousand), followed by fuel and oil ($4.7 thousand), vessel repair and maintenance ($3.0 thousand), loan payments ($2.9 thousand), tackle and supply expenses ($1.8 thousand), and expenses for a hired captain ($1.2 thousand). Other expenses included crew payments ($920), bait ($833), investments ($596), ice ($172), and groceries ($135).

In 2010, the average head-boat owner's net cash flow was $95.2 thousand (Table 13). Inflows totaled $213.5 thousand for an average vessel. The largest expenditure for the average head-boat vessel was fuel and oil ($24.8 thousand), followed by crew ($18.2 thousand) and hired captain ($17.0 thousand) expenses, overhead ($16.0 thousand), loan payments ($14.4 thousand), vessel repair and maintenance ($8.8 thousand), insurance ($6.7 thousand), bait ($5.5 thousand), and tackle and supply expenses ($3.9 thousand). Average investment expenditures were $1.3 thousand and other expenses included groceries ($289) and ice ($195).

3.5.3. Total Cash Flow in Northeast

Survey results and MRIP data were used to quantify the total costs and earnings of all Northeast charter and head boat businesses in 2010. First, survey data were used to calculate revenues, expenses, and net returns for the "average" charter and the "average" head boat in 2010 (Tables 12 and 13). Average cash flow values, by type of vessel, were then multiplied separately by the total number of unique active charter (3,698) and head boats (178) estimated to have taken passengers for-hire in 2010 across all of the Northeast coastal states. The MRIP For-Hire Vessel Directory provided the data necessary to determine the number of unique charter and head boats active during some portion of 2010.[7] The product of the average values and the number of unique charter and head boats provides an estimate of the total cash flow for the Northeast for-hire fleet in 2010 (Table 14). In 2010, the total for-hire fleet in the Northeast obtained over $140 million in gross revenue (i.e., sales receipts). Operating expenses exceeded $104 million (including wages and salaries paid to employees), and net returns to owners (i.e., net profits) were approximately $36 million.

3.6. Economic Contribution

The economic contribution of the for-hire fleet to the overall economy in the Northeast extends well beyond simply measuring the direct employment, income, and gross revenues of the for-hire businesses. For-hire businesses purchase products and services to maintain and operate their vessels, and businesses supplying products and services must pay employees and buy products and services from their suppliers. These secondary suppliers, in turn, purchase products and services from their own suppliers, triggering further indirect multiplier effects that are dependent upon the initial demands of the for-hire fleet. This cascading series of industry-toindustry multiplier effects and the cycle of consumption spending induced by all the incomes generated in these economic activities contribute to the economy's employment and income base and continues until all of the goods and services are sourced from outside the Northeast.

3.6.1. Regional Input-output Assessment

An analytical framework known as regional input-output analysis can be used to measure indirect and induced multiplier effects and thus estimate the total contribution of a particular industry sector to the overall regional economy. The input-output modeling approach provides a snapshot of the universe of linkages between the economic sectors of an economy and is generally described as a static general equilibrium approach to quantitative economic analysis. For a comprehensive description of the input-output modeling technique, see Miller and Blair (1985).

In the assessment provided here, a ready-made regional input-output system called IMPLAN (Minnesota IMPLAN Group, Inc) was used to estimate the amount that for-hire businesses contribute to the Northeast's economy as measured by total employment, labor income, and sales. Employment represents the estimated number of total wage and salary employees (both full and part-time), as well as self-employed workers in the region and is expressed as total jobs. Labor income represents all forms of employment income, including employee compensation (wages and benefits) and self-employed income earned in the region. Sales reflect the estimated annual dollar value of production in the region summed across all industries and is a measure of total economic activity.

Regionwide "indirect" multiplier effects were estimated by multiplying the value of each of the individual expense items that was spent by the for-hire fleet within the region by the corresponding IMPLAN-generated multiplier. IMPLAN multipliers measure the total sales, income, and employment in each economic sector within the region caused by $1 in sales in any particular sector. Therefore, the product of the expenditure values that are spent within the region with their matching IMPLAN-generated multiplier provides an estimate of the contribution of each particular expenditure item to the regional economy.

Income earned by vessel owners, captains, crew/mates, and office personnel contributes additional economic effects to the Northeast's economy through the mix of products and services purchased from businesses located in the region. IMPLAN multipliers were also used to calculate these "induced" contributions. The full contribution of the for-hire fleet to the overall regional economy in the Northeast was then measured by adding the fleet expenditure contributions (indirect effects) and the personal consumption expenditure contributions (induced effects) to the estimated sales, income, and employment of the for-hire fleet in 2010 (direct effects). A detailed account of the IMPLAN modeling approach is provided in Appendix V.

3.6.2. Contribution Assessment Results

The economic contribution of the charter and head boat fleet to the overall regional economy in the Northeast is summarized in Table 15. In 2010, charter and head boat activities contributed an estimated $334.0 million in total sales to Northeast businesses, $116.9 million in total income to individuals working in the Northeast and supported 7,530 Northeast jobs (full and part-time).

The economic contribution of charter boats was higher than the contribution of head boats across all three economic measures. The multiplier relationships between the operation of charter and head boat businesses and the supporting regional economy were similar but, because of the large difference in the estimated number of active vessels in the two fleets (178 head boats vs. 3,698 charter boats) overall charter boat expenditures and net returns were considerably higher.

The total contribution of the for-hire fleet by industry type is shown in Table 16. In 2010, the for-hire fleet grossed $140.3 million in sales, provided $50.4 million in income to owners, hired captains, crew/mates, and office staff, and employed over 6,200 individuals in the Northeast. The multiplier effects of this activity were substantial. The for-hire industry supported an additional $193.7 million in sales, $66.5 million in income, and 1,290 jobs in other industries in the Northeast. Service businesses (real estate, food services, marinas, repair shops, etc.), wholesale and retail trade businesses (sporting goods stores, bait shops, gas stations, etc.), and manufacturing businesses (fishing gear manufactures, fuel refineries, commercial fishermen [bait], etc.) were the enterprises most dependent on the for-hire fleet. Over 700 service sector jobs, 360 wholesale and retail trade jobs, and 63 manufacturing jobs were supported by the for-hire fleet in the Northeast in 2010.

In terms of employment, the top ten industries supported by the for-hire fleet are shown in Table 17. Following employment in the for-hire industry itself, the highest number of jobs were in wholesale trade (74), recreation services (marinas; 72), marine supply stores (69), food services (69), sporting goods (57), commercial fishing (bait; 54), real estate (46), gasoline stations (41), and private hospitals (37).

4. DISCUSSION

4.1. Study Design

The study design was stratified across two types of for-hire vessels: charter and head boats. However, based on comments received during the pretesting stage, the survey asked respondents to indicate whether a particular vessel was a charter boat, a head boat, or a guide boat. A guide boat was defined as a for-hire fishing boat that carries four or fewer individuals and mostly fishes in near shore and inshore waters, including bays and inlets. The operator must also have, at a minimum, a USCG operator license to carry six or fewer passengers. Because of sampling issues, we included guide boats within the charter boat category, but based on the percentage of vessels classified as guide boats from our survey, we recommend that future for-hire studies should distinguish between operations classified as "charter" and those classified as "guide." Twenty-four percent (n=67) of the vessels in our charter boat group were self-identified as guide boats.

Three methods were used to collect data from for-hire owners: personal interviews, mail surveys, and telephone surveys. Analysis of Variance (ANOVA) tests were conducted to evaluate differences in means for statistical significance across the three data collection vehicles. Tests were conducted using the GLM procedure in SAS, which can be used to perform analysis of variance tests on unbalanced data sets. There were unequal numbers of observations in each survey treatment group because the number of telephone-completed surveys was considerably lower than those completed through personal interviews or by mail. ANOVA tests were only performed on financial data collected from for-hire owners.

No significant differences in means were found across any of the financial variables except for outstanding loan payments (i.e., liabilities) by charter boat owners (Table 18). This result reflected a few relatively high liability payments by charter boat owners reporting over the phone. Removal of these records from the data set had little effect on estimated mean liability payments by charter boat owners, and therefore these records were left in the data set. Overall, no significant differences were found across the three survey approaches employed in this study.

4.2. Economic Status of the for-Hire Industry

The survey results show that the overall financial condition of marine recreational for-hire fishing businesses in the Northeast is mixed. Assets exceed liabilities by over four times for the average charter and head boat, and over 90% of charter and head boat owners carry insurance coverage. This implies that a rather strong financial for-hire fishing fleet exists in the Northeast. The results also reveal that the average charter boat produced only a little over $5.1 thousand in net income in 2010, and over half of the charter boats in the Northeast actually incurred higher expenses than revenues in 2010. However, the margin of error in our estimate of average charter boat net income is large. The confidence intervals indicate that we can only be 95% certain that the true average charter boat net income is between -$2.9 thousand to $13.6 thousand. In contrast to the average charter boat, the average head boat generated over $95.1 thousand in net income in 2010 although median net income per head boat was lower at $50.1 thousand.

The estimated low level of earnings for the average charter vessel in 2010 is likely due to a variety of reasons. First, Northeast for-hire businesses are highly seasonal, so overall earnings are somewhat limited by a short fishing season. The short fishing season probably explains why charter boat owners, on average, earned only about 17% of their total 2010 income from their charter boat business. The survey data further indicate that only 5% of charter boat owners earned 100% of their annual income in 2010 from their charter activities. Some for-hire owners indicated that passenger levels were lower in 2010 because of the economy, and many owners (particularly charter boat owners) indicated that they operated the business mainly for lifestyle benefits; that is, charter employment has more to do with lifestyle choices than financial considerations. The idea that owners operate charter boats for the lifestyle has also been noted in other studies of charter boat owners (Liese and Carter, 2011).

Second, in addition to taking passengers for-hire, some charter boat owners also use their boats for nonfinancial purposes (pleasure cruising, sightseeing, recreational fishing without paying passengers, etc.). Because the economic survey obtained expenditure information on total annual operating costs in 2010, the operating costs associated with uses of the vessel that do not produce income would have been included in the expense estimates provided by charter boat owners. As a result, estimated operating costs in 2010 are based on total vessel activity, while gross revenues are calculated from only a portion of the total vessel activity of multiple-use vessels.

Third, business tax deductions and depreciation were not considered in the calculation of net earnings. Profits earned by for-hire owners eligible for deductions, credits, and/or depreciation in 2010 would have been higher than indicated by our results. Hence, our estimate of average net returns per charter vessel ($5,175) should likely be considered a lower bound approximation.

As well, there is considerable variation in the financial characteristics of for-hire operations, even after accounting for differences between charter boats and head boats. As is apparent in the balance sheet and cash flow results, owner's equity and net cash flow have rather large ranges. Furthermore, for some cost categories (particularly for charter boats) $0 is reported as the median result. This is not unusual for cost and earnings surveys of fishing vessels and indicates that at least 50% of the respondents did not have costs in these categories, therefore the median becomes 0.

The overall cost and earnings results for the Northeast for-hire fleet are similar to other recent regional studies of for-hire fleets. Owner's equity averaged $30 – 60 thousand in 2009 for charter boats in the Gulf of Mexico, depending on the Gulf State (Savolainen et al. 2012). In 2010, the average charter boat equity in Northeast was $48 thousand. The average head boat equity in the Gulf of Mexico was $165 – 220 thousand in 2009 (Savolainen et al. 2012), while the average Northeast head boat owner's equity in 2010 was $161 thousand. Cash flow in the Gulf of Mexico charter boat fleet was $15 – 40 thousand in 2009, depending on the state, while head boat cash flow was approximately $70 thousand (Savolainen et al. 2012). In comparison, the average Northeast charter boat owner's cash flow in 2010 was slightly over $5 thousand, and the average head boat owner's cash flow in 2010 was $95 thousand. In another study of the Southeast for-hire fleet, annual net revenue was $2 thousand in 2003, not including crew costs (Liese and Carter, 2011).

Our input-output results show that a substantial number of jobs are directly and indirectly dependent upon the for-hire industry in the Northeast. An estimated 7,530 jobs in the overall Northeast regional economy were supported by the active for-hire fleet in 2010. The actual number of jobs supported by for-hire fishing activity in the Northeast is certainly higher, as the modeling results reported here are conservative in that they only measure the contribution of the for-hire industry itself to the Northeast's economy. Auxiliary expenditures by for-hire passengers, while traveling to and from the for-hire fishing site (e.g., auto fuel, lodging, food, bait, tackle, or equipment not included as part of the passenger fees) also contribute to the economy's employment and income base. The contribution of these auxiliary expenditures by passengers was not included in this assessment. A case could be made that the total contribution of the for-hire industry to the Northeast's economy should also include the multiplier effects of these auxiliary expenditures by for-hire passengers. Additionally, for-hire boats that primarily target offshore HMS (billfish, swordfish, tunas, sharks, wahoo, dolphin, and amberjack) were not included in this study. Although the number of for-hire boats operating in the Northeast that primarily target HMS is unknown, our results would certainly be larger if the multiplier effects of these boats were also measured.

ACKNOWLEDGMENTS

This study would not have been possible without the assistance of almost three hundred charter and head boat owners who took the time to diligently complete a rather long survey about the financial operations of their businesses. The willingness of these individuals to participate in this study demonstrates the importance that the survey participants place on obtaining economic data about their profession.

Secondly, we would like to thank members of the Northeast Charter Boat Captain's Association, the Rhode Island Party and Charter Association, the Montauk Boatmen's and Captain's Association, the Upper Bay (Chesapeake) Charter Captain's Association, and the Coastal Conservation Association of Maryland for providing comments and/or suggestions on early versions of the economic survey.

We thank the Gentner Consulting Group (GCG) who assisted with the overall design of the study, attended for-hire association meetings to explain the study, and tested early versions of the survey. GCG also conducted individual pretests with many owners and captains to ensure the survey was both comprehensive and sensible.

We also thank the many individuals involved at QuanTech Inc. Their professionalism and desire to develop, administer, and collect the best data possible was clearly evident.

Finally, we thank Christopher Liese, Matthew McPherson, Fred Serchuk, and Jarita Davis for providing many insightful comments and suggestions on previous versions of this paper.

REFERENCES

Dillman DA. 2000. Mail and internet surveys: The tailored design method, Wiley, New York (Second Edition).

Dumas CF, Whitehead JC, Landry CE, Herstine JH. 2009. Economic impacts and recreation value of the North Carolina for-hire fishing fleet. North Carolina Sea Grant, Fishery Resource Grant Report 07-FEG-05.

Holland SM, Oh CO, Larkin SL, Hodges AW. 2012. The operations and economics of the for-hire fishing fleets of the south Atlantic states and the Atlantic Coast of Florida. University of Florida contract report prepared for the National Marine Fisheries Service.

Liese C, Carter DW. 2011. Collecting economic data from the for-hire fishing sector: Lessons from a cost and earnings survey of the southeast U.S. charter boat industry. 14 p. In Beard TD Jr, Loftus AJ, Arlinghaus R (editors). The Angler and the Environment. American Fisheries Society, Bethesda, MD.

Liese C, Travis M. 2010. The annual economic survey of federal gulf shrimp permit holders: Implementation and descriptive results for 2008. NOAA Technical Memorandum NMFSSEFSC-601.

Savolainen MA, Caffey RH, Kazmierczak RF Jr. 2012. Economic and attitudinal perspectives of the recreational for-hire industry in the U.S. Gulf of Mexico [master's thesis]. Center for Natural Resource Economics and Policy, Department of Agricultural Economics and Agribusiness, Louisiana State University.

Watson P, Wilson J, Thilmany D, Winter S. 2007. Determining economic contributions and impacts: what is the difference and why do we care? Journal of Regional Analysis and Policy, 37(2): 140-146.

Table 1. For-hire organizations contacted during outreach

Organization	Provided survey design assistance
Northeast Charter Boat Captain's Association	√
Rhode Island Party and Charter Association	√
Montauk Boatmen's and Captain's Association	√
Upper Bay (Chesapeake) Charter Captain's Association	√
Coastal Conservation Association (CCA) of MD	√
Maryland Charter Boat Association	
Virginia Charter Boat Association	
National Association of Charter Boat Operators	

Table 2. Number of vessels with telephone numbers and addresses selected for the RFHES from the for-hire survey vessel directory, by state and vessel type

	Vessel type		
State	Charter boat	Head boat	All
CT	70	5	75
DE	35	8	43
ME	63	3	66
MD	167	12	179
MA	406	24	430
NH	29	11	40
NJ	233	43	276

Table 2. (Continued)

State	Vessel type		All
	Charter boat	Head boat	
NY	135	37	172
NC	232	11	243
RI	92	4	96
VA	44	12	56
All	1,506	170	1,676

Table 3. Results of RFHES screening calls

	Screener Dialing Status												
	Eligible, agreed to participate		Could not be contacted		Ineligible		Did not own for-hire vessel		Refusal		Wrong/bad number		All
	No.	%	No.	%	No.	%	No.	%	No.	%	No.	%	No.
CT	18	24.00	28	37.33	19	25.33	1	1.33	6	8.00	3	4.00	75
DE	12	27.91	10	23.26	8	18.60	1	2.33	11	25.58	1	2.33	43
ME	34	51.52	13	19.70	13	19.70	0	0.00	5	7.58	1	1.52	66
MD	29	16.20	33	18.44	40	22.35	8	4.47	46	25.70	23	12.85	179
MA	78	18.14	114	26.51	151	35.12	7	1.63	56	13.02	24	5.58	430
NH	5	12.50	18	45.00	9	22.50	0	0.00	5	12.50	3	7.50	40
NJ	55	19.93	94	34.06	49	17.75	6	2.17	41	14.86	31	11.23	276
NY	41	23.84	48	27.91	43	25.00	4	2.33	21	12.21	15	8.72	172
NC	54	22.22	60	24.69	66	27.16	9	3.70	35	14.40	19	7.82	243
RI	24	25.00	26	27.08	22	22.92	2	2.08	13	13.54	9	9.38	96
VA	17	30.36	17	30.36	12	21.43	0	0.00	9	16.07	1	1.79	56
All	367	21.90	461	27.51	432	25.78	38	2.27	248	14.80	130	7.76	1,676

Table 4. Survey results for contacted respondents

	Agreed to do survey								Vessels profiled		
	Completed survey in-person		Completed survey phone		Completed survey mail/email		Never completed Survey		Charter	Head boat	All
	No.	%	No.	%	No.	%	No.	%	No.	No.	No.
CT	8	18.60	1	2.33	8	18.60	1	2.33	15	1	16
DE	6	19.35	0	0.00	4	12.90	2	6.45	11	1	12
ME	13	25.00	9	17.31	10	19.23	2	3.85	35	0	35
MD	15	13.04	1	0.87	10	8.70	3	2.61	24	9	33
MA	24	8.42	5	1.75	30	10.53	19	6.67	61	5	66

	Agreed to do survey							Vessels profiled		
	Completed survey in-person		Completed survey phone		Completed survey mail/email		Never completed Survey		Charter	Head boat	All
	No.	%	No.	%	No.	%	No.	%	No.	No.	No.
NH	1	5.26	3	15.79	0	0.00	1	5.26	0	3	3
NJ	20	13.79	2	1.38	21	14.48	12	8.28	39	10	49
NY	15	14.29	1	0.95	14	13.33	11	10.48	23	12	35
NC	24	15.48	0	0.00	16	10.32	14	9.03	43	1	44
RI	8	13.56	2	3.39	10	16.95	4	6.78	19	4	23
VA	7	18.42	0	0.00	7	18.42	3	7.89	9	7	16
All	141	13.47	24	2.29	130	12.42	72	6.88	279	53	332

Table 5. Vessel characteristics by operating class

	Charter	Head boat
Vessel characteristics	Mean	
Length (ft)	29.40	63.38
Horsepower	363.2	875.56
Passenger capacity	8.94	90.65
Year built	1995	1979
Year vessel purchased	2003	1997
Purchased new *(% yes)*	40.94%	30.43%
Purchase price ($'s)	79,305	228,454
Number of crew (in season)		
Full-time	0.18	1.95
Part-time	0.52	1.54
Hull material		
Wood	6%	56%
Fiberglass	88%	27%
Aluminum	4%	18%
Steel	1%	0%
Other	1%	0%
Location		
Docked/moored	76%	100%
Trailered	24%	0%

Table 6. Vessel operations by operating class

Vessel operation	Charter	Head boat
	Percent	
Ownership type		
Owner/operator	97.07%	64.44%
Owner/nonoperator	1.83%	24.44%
Paid captain, private	0.37%	2.22%
Paid captain, corporate	0.73%	8.88%
Business structure		
Sole proprietorship	63.00%	5%
Partnership	1.10%	0%
Corporation	13.55%	76%
LLC	20.88%	17%
Other	1.47%	2%
Nonfishing trips		
Bait catching trips (without patrons)	46.01%	6.52%
Number of trips *(mean)*	8.92	8.33
Length of bait trips *(mean hours)*	2.91	3
Trips to scout locations (without patrons)	68.48%	34.88%
Number of trips *(mean)*	9.96	2.67
Length of scout trips *(mean hours)*	4.80	5
Other nonfishing trips - sightseeing, whale watching, etc.	49.28%	60.47%
Number of trips *(mean)*	4	24

Table 7. Owner characteristics by operating class

Owner characteristics	Charter	Head boat
	Mean	
Age of owner	52.2	56.7
Years of experience as owner/captain	14.2	24.8
Percent of total annual gross income earned from for-hire fishing activities	17%	70%

Table 8. Vessel trip types by operating class

	Charter	Head boat
% Offering half day trips	85%	74%
Number of half day trips	26	203
January – March	0.4	0.0
April – June	7.4	58.3
July – September	15.1	129.8
October – December	3.4	15.0
Number of trips donated to charity	1.2	2.7
Typical length of trip (hrs)	4.7	4.4
Average number of passengers	4.3	26.6
Percent of trips in Federal waters	14%	15%
Revenue earned on a typical trip	$450.15[a]	$31.92[b]
% Offering full day trips	90%	72%
Number of full day trips	19	69
January – March	0.5	1.5
April – June	5.7	28.1
July – September	9.7	26.4
October – December	3.3	13.4
Number of trips donated to charity	0.4	1.7
Typical length of trip (hrs)	8.5	8.3
Average number of passengers	4.8	20.6
Percent of trips in Federal waters	34%	39%
Revenue earned on a typical trip	$707.36[a]	$91.36[b]
% Offering overnight trips	13%	12%
Number of overnight trips	2	11
January – March	0.0	0.0
April – June	0.3	1.8
July – September	1.4	6.8
October – December	0.1	2.8
Number of trips donated to charity	0.0	0.0
Typical length of trip (hrs)	23.3	24.4
Average number of passengers	5.4	19.2
Percent of trips in Federal waters	63%	100%
Revenue earned on a typical trip	$1,914.25[a]	$287.80[b]
% Offering other trips	26%	23%
Number of other trips	10	34
January – March	0.2	0.0

Table 8. (Continued)

	Charter	Head boat
April – June	2.0	6.4
July – September	6.4	20.4
October – December	1.1	7.5
Number of trips donated to charity	0.3	0.1
Typical length of trip (hrs)	7.5	9.5
Average number of passengers	4.6	32.4
Percent of trips in Federal waters	32%	54%
Revenue earned on a typical trip	$520.38[a]	$72.94[b]

[a] This refers to the fee charged for the entire boat on a charter boat trip.
[b] This refers to the fee charged per person on a head boat trip.

Table 9. Cost and earnings of an average charter vessel in 2010

	Mean	Standard deviation	Population mean 95% confidence interval Lower	Population mean 95% confidence interval Upper	Median
Balance sheet (end of 2010)					
Assets - Market value of vessel	65,009	82,024	55,170	74,848	40,000
Purchase price	74,256	92,480	63,385	85,127	42,000
Liabilities - Outstanding loans					
Loan on vessel	16,008	35,564	11,509	20,507	0
Short term operating loan	762	4,303	219	1,305	0
Outstanding vessel loans (%)	*(30%)*				
Operating loans (%)	*(6%)*				
Equity - Owner's equity in vessel	48,423[a]	81,062	38,588	58,258	25,000
Insurance coverage (%)	*(91%)*				

[a] The subtraction of mean liabilities from mean assets provides a slightly different estimate of mean equity because of differences in the number of observations used in the calculations.

Table 10. Cost and earnings of an average head boat in 2010

	Mean	Standard deviation	Population mean 95% confidence interval Lower	Population mean 95% confidence interval Upper	Median
Balance Sheet (end of 2010)					
Assets - Market value of vessel	241,750	196,383	145,046	338,454	165,000
Purchase price	265,949	312,045	170,432	361,466	170,000
Liabilities - Outstanding loans					
Loan on vessel	59,420	118,683	18,926	99,914	0
Short term operating loan	3,641	8,977	531	6,751	0
Outstanding vessel loans (%)	*(45%)*				
Operating loans (%)	*(19%)*				
Equity - Owner's equity in vessel	160,828[a]	186,441	96,229	225,427	100,000
Insurance coverage (%)	*(90%)*				

[a] The subtraction of mean liabilities from mean assets provides a slightly different estimate of mean equity because of differences in the number of observations used in the calculations.

Table 11. Annual cash flow description of revenues, expenses and net returns

Cash flow category	Description
Inflow (gross revenue)	Income from passenger fees, tips / fish cleaning, sale of food and beverages, souvenirs, sale of fish, secondary income from commercial fishing, other nonfishing activities such as whale watching trips, bird watching, sunset cruises, burials at sea, etc.
Outflow (expenses)	
Fuel and oil	Fuel and oil
Bait	Bait
Ice	Ice
Food and drink	Food and drink

Table 11. (Continued)

Cash flow category	Description
Tackle and supplies	Fishing gear and tackle, other supplies (soap, detergent, mops, brooms, bags, uniforms/clothes, trash bags, other plastic bags)
Repair and maintenance Insurance	By boatyard, by staff Insurance
Overhead	Office staff, state fishing permits, federal fishing permits, fishing association dues, professional certifications, accounting / bookkeeping, bank fees, legal fees, advertising and promotion, booking agent fees, dock slip fees, telephone and internet, electric electric and other utilities, weather service subscriptions, company vehicle lease, company vehicle maintenance
Hired captain	Wages / salaries paid to hired captains
Crew / mates	Wages / salaries paid to crew
Investments	Investments in new electronics
Loan Payments	Principal and interest
Owner net returns	Inflow (gross revenue) - outflow (expenditures)

Table 12. Annual cash flow of an average charter vessel

	Mean	Standard deviation	Population mean 95% confidence interval Lower	Population mean 95% confidence interval Upper	Median
Annual cash flow					
Inflow - Gross revenue	27,650	65,846	19,159	36,141	13,450
Outflow - Expenditures					
Fuel and oil	4,661	5,636	3,928	5,394	3,000
Bait	833	1,688	616	1,050	250
Ice	172	292	135	209	50
Food and drink	135	364	89	181	0
Tackle and supplies	1,798	2,214	1,516	2,080	1,000
Repair and maintenance	2,978	4,701	2,378	3,578	1,500
Insurance	1,500	1,203	1,347	1,653	1,200

	Mean	Standard deviation	Population mean 95% confidence interval		Median
			Lower	Upper	
Overhead	4,887	3,955	4,348	5,426	4,255
Hired Captain	1,169	4,451	589	1,749	0
Per paid captain	*[8,258]*				
Crew/mate	920	2,818	560	1,280	0
Per paid crew/mate	*[1,094]*				
Investments	596	1,394	418	774	0
Loan payments	2,906	4,973	2,278	3,534	0
Net cash flow	5,175[a]	62,336	-2,916	13,266	-595

[a] The subtraction of mean outflows from mean inflows provides a slightly different estimate of mean net cash flow because of differences in the number of observations used in the calculations.

Table 13. Annual cash flow of an average head boat vessel

	Mean	Standard deviation	Population mean 95% confidence interval		Median
			Lower	Upper	
Annual Cash Flow					
Inflow - Gross revenue	213,549	131,080	163,163	263,935	192,420
Outflow - Expenditures					
Fuel and oil	24,775	16,669	17,809	31,741	24,000
Bait	5,498	4,148	3,872	7,124	5,000
Ice	195	370	53	337	0
Food and drink	289	675	34	544	0
Tackle and supplies	3,926	3,597	2,639	5,213	2,750
Repair and maintenance	8,832	9,203	5,482	12,182	6,000
Insurance	6,709	4,247	5,044	8,374	8,000
Overhead	16,042	11,299	12,064	20,020	16,780
Hired Captain	17,014	18,031	10,083	23,945	15,000
Per paid captain	*[27,648]*				

Table 13. (Continued)

	Mean	Standard deviation	Population mean 95% confidence interval Lower	Population mean 95% confidence interval Upper	Median
Crew/mate	18,239	21,168	10,254	26,224	12,000
Per paid crew/mate	*[5,042]*				
Investments	1,339	1,996	625	2,053	317
Loan payments	14,352	18,941	7,889	20,815	6,000
Net cash flow	95,183[a]	122,968	47,916	142,450	50,106

[a] The subtraction of mean outflows from mean inflows provides a slightly different estimate of mean net cash flow because of differences in the number of observations used in the calculations.

Table 14. Total 2010 cash flow for charter and head boats in the Northeast ($1,000)

	Charter	Head boat	Total
Inflow (gross revenue)	102,250	38,012	140,261
Outflow (expenses)			
Fuel and oil	17,236	4,410	21,646
Bait	3,080	979	4,059
Ice	636	35	671
Food and drink	499	51	551
Tackle and supplies	6,649	699	7,348
Repair and maintenance	11,013	1,572	12,585
Insurance	5,547	1,194	6,741
Overhead	18,072	2,855	20,928
Hired captain	4,323	3,028	7,351
Crew / mates	3,402	3,247	6,649
Investments	2,204	238	2,442
Loan Payments	10,746	2,555	13,301
Owner net returns	19,034[a]	16,943	35,976

[a] The subtraction of mean outflows from mean inflows provides a slightly different estimate of mean net cash flow because of differences in the number of observations used in the calculations.

Table 15. Total sales, labor income, and employment contributions of the for-hire fishing fleet to the Northeast's economy (Maine - North Carolina)

	Sales ($1,000)	Economic Contribution Income ($1,000)	Jobs (full and part-time)
Charter	247,914	76,925	6,589
Head boat	86,085	39,966	941
Total	333,999	116,891	7,530

Table 16. Total economic contribution by industry type (charter and head boats combined)

Industry Type	Sales ($1,000)	Income ($1,000)	Jobs (full and part-time)
For-hire fleet (charter and head boats)	140,261	50,350	6,240
Agriculture	3,177	1,004	59
Mining	576	132	1
Construction	1,012	498	9
Manufacturing	25,444	4,799	63
Transportation, communications, and public utilities	20,088	5,317	62
Retail and wholesale trade	35,291	16,059	360
Services	104,576	36,664	708
Government	3,573	2,068	28
Total	333,999	116,891	7,530

Table 17. Employment Supported by For-Hire Activity in the Northeast: Top Ten Industries

Rank	Industry	Jobs (full and part-time)
1	For-hire fleet	6,240
2	Wholesale trade businesses	74
3	Amusement parks, arcades, and gambling industries (marinas)	72

Table 17. (Continued)

Rank	Industry	Jobs (full and part-time)
4	Retail stores - motor vehicle and parts (boat parts)	69
5	Food services and drinking places	69
6	Retail stores - sporting goods (bait retail, tackle and gear)	57
7	Commercial fishing (bait suppliers)	54
8	Real estate establishments	46
9	Retail stores - gasoline stations	41
10	Private hospitals	37

Table 18. Analysis of variance tests for differences in means among survey types (GLM manova procedure in SAS

	Charter boats		Head boats	
	F Value	Pr > F	F Value	Pr > F
Balance sheet (end of 2010)				
Assets – Market value of vessel	0.670	0.511	0.221	0.804
Liabilities - Outstanding loans	3.501	0.032[a]	1.480	0.233
Equity - Owner's equity in vessel	0.710	0.494	0.643	0.429
Annual cash flow				
Inflow - Gross revenue	1.021	0.361	0.752	0.396
Outflow - Expenditures	0.530	0.588	0.694	0.513
Net cash flow	0.640	0.528	0.152	0.701

[a]Significance at the 95% level.

6. APPENDICES

6.1. Appendix I: Advance Letter to Survey Respondents

Name
Street address
City, State, Zip

Month Day, Year

Dear Name,

Now is the time to demonstrate the economic importance of charter boats and head boats. The National Marine Fisheries Service (NMFS) currently has no data on the economic performance of your industry. Lack of data makes it impossible to show the New England and Mid-Atlantic Fishery Management Councils just how important you are to the economic health of your coastal community, or to accurately assess the economic impact fisheries policies have on your industry and community. The 2011 Recreational For-Hire Economic Survey (RFHES) aims to change that and we need your help. Please join us in this critical effort to establish your industry's economic importance by participating in the survey.

The enclosed RFHES questionnaire and FAQs were developed and tested with the assistance of for-hire boat captains and owners like you. Our interviewers will be calling you in the next two weeks to determine your eligibility for the survey and to request an in-person interview. We understand the confidential nature of the information sought and will take all appropriate steps to protect your privacy. We know your time is valuable, but hope you will agree to participate. A small token of appreciation is enclosed as a way of saying thanks for your help.

QuanTech is conducting the RFHES under a contract with NOAA's Northeast Fisheries Science Center, the research arm of NOAA Fisheries in the region. For more information, please contact:

Scott Steinback	Daemian Schreiber
Economist, Social Sciences Branch	Program Manager,
	Fisheries Research Group
Northeast Fisheries Science Center	QuanTech, Inc., Arlington, Virginia
Office: 508-495-2371	Office: 703-312-7831
Email: scott.steinback@noaa.gov	Email: dschreiber@quantech.com

Sincerely,
Dr. David C. Cox
President, QuanTech

6.2. Appendix II: Frequently Asked Questions and Answers for Respondents

Recreational for-Hire Economic Survey

Frequently Asked Questions (FAQS) and Answers

Why is this survey being conducted?

The recreational for-hire industry is economically important up and down the East Coast. However, NMFS currently lacks the data to adequately estimate the economic impacts of changes in fishery regulations on this industry. The Recreational For-Hire Economic Survey (RFHES) is necessary to demonstrate the overall economic importance of the industry and to gauge how policies impact the economic health of head boat and charter fishing operations in New England and the Mid Atlantic (all coastal states from North Carolina north to Maine). This survey will collect financial data including trip and annual costs and revenue. The data will be used to create an economic impact model of the head boat and charter fishing industry. This economic impact model will be used to estimate the overall economic importance of the entire for-hire industry. Additionally, the model will be used to examine how changes in policy positively or negatively impact this important industry.

Who is conducting the survey?

The survey is funded by the National Marine Fisheries Service (NMFS) and is being conducted by QuanTech, Inc. of Arlington, Virginia. Survey design and testing was completed by Gentner Consulting. QuanTech's interviewers will conduct the actual in-person interviews.

How was I selected and is my participation voluntary?

You were selected randomly from the 2010 NMFS for-hire telephone survey (FHTS) directory, which is compiled from State and Federal permit lists. Your participation in this survey is voluntary.

How long will it take to complete the survey?

The survey designers aimed for a survey that takes no longer than one hour to complete. If you own a single boat and only offer one type of trip (half day, full day, or overnight), the survey will be quite short, taking only about 20 minutes.

Why am I being asked to provide economic information?

By providing information about your business, you are helping to construct a baseline assessment of the financial health and economic impact of the recreational for-hire industry. Knowing the industry's profitability and economic value is especially important when benefits and costs of new regulations are discussed by policy makers. The information is also important when determining the economic effects of other external forces, such as economic downturns, fuel prices, and natural disasters. Such information is commonly requested by decision makers and media outlets interested in publicizing the industry's economic situation. Currently, it is impossible to answer these questions due to lack of data.

Will the IRS get any of my information?

No. As fisheries economists, we are only interested in collecting appropriate data to provide an accurate snapshot of the recreational for-hire industry as a whole. Individual data is treated as confidential. When you complete your interview, identifying information will be removed from the rest of your answers and will not be submitted to NMFS.

Will my answers remain anonymous?

Yes. All individual information will be treated as strictly confidential. Individual data will be combined with information from other respondents to present an overall view of the economic health of the industry or a particular component of the industry.

6.3. Appendix III: Final Survey Instrument

2011 Recreational for-Hire Economic Survey (RFHES)

Screening Introduction:

May I please speak to [NAME OF CONTACT]?
Hello, this is [INTERVIEWER] calling on behalf of NOAA Fisheries and the For-Hire
ECONOMIC Survey.
Are you/ is [NAME OF CONTACT] the owner of [VESSEL NAME]?
IF "YES", CONTINUE TO SURVEY DESCRIPTION 1.
IF "NO", CONTINUE TO SURVEY DESCRIPTION 2.

Survey Description 1:

We recently mailed you a package about an important economic survey. We're surveying owners of charter and head boats to collect economic data needed to evaluate the economic importance of the for-hire fishery. The [VESSEL NAME] has been selected at random from a directory of charter and head boats to be included in this study. I would like to ask a few questions about the vessel to determine its eligibility. If we determine that the vessel is eligible for the study, we will contact you again to schedule an in-person interview. This data will remain confidential and this survey is being conducted in accordance with the Privacy Act of 1974, therefore your participation is voluntary. **[CONTINUE]**

1. Did the [VESSEL NAME] take anyone fishing for a fee in 2010?
    a. Yes **[CONTINUE]**
    b. No **[VESSEL IS NOT ELIGIBLE, TERMINATE]**
2. Did more than 50% of the [VESSEL NAME]'s for-hire trips in 2010 target highly migratory species (tunas, sharks, billfish, or swordfish)?
    a. Yes **[VESSEL IS NOT ELIGIBLE, TERMINATE]**
    b. No **[CONTINUE]**
3. The [VESSEL NAME] meets the eligibility requirements for this study. Are you willing to provide cost and earnings information associated with your for-hire fishing business?
    a. Yes **[CONTINUE]**
    b. No **[TRY TO CONVERT REFUSAL]**
4. One of our in-person interviewers will call you back to schedule an appointment. Our interviewer will meet you at a time and location that you designate. The best way to schedule the appointment is if the interviewer calls you directly. What is the best time for the interviewer to call you back? **[ENTER BEST TIME TO CALL, THEN TERMINATE]**

Survey Description 2:

We recently mailed you a package about an important economic survey. We're surveying owners of charter and head boats to collect economic data needed to evaluate the economic importance of the for-hire fishery. The [VESSEL NAME] has been selected at random from a directory of charter and head boats to be included in this study. Could you provide the name and telephone number of the person who can provide cost and earnings information for the [VESSEL NAME]?

    a. Yes **[ENTER NAME AND TELEPHONE NUMBER, THEN TERMINATE]**
    b. No **[TERMINATE]**

Questionnaire:

Vessel Characteristics
1. How many boats in each of following categories do you own?

    a. _____ **guide boats** *(A guide boat is a for-hire fishing boat that carries 4 or less and mostly fishes near shore, inshore, bays, and inlet, operator must have, at a minimum, a USCG operator license to carry 6 or fewer passengers on near shore and inland waters.)*

    b. _____ **6 pack charter boats** *(6 passenger charter boat is an uninspected for-hire fishing vessel that carries 6 persons or fewer and mostly fishes offshore and inshore waters. The operator must possess ,at a minimum, a USCG license to carry 6 or fewer passengers in offshore waters.)*

    c. _____ **overload charter boats** *(Overload or multi-passenger charter boat is a vessel that has a USCG Certificate of Inspection (COI) to carry a specified number of passengers with a specified navigation route. This vessel generally charges a fee for the vessel up to a specified number and may charge an additional fee for each passenger over the specified amount. The operator must possess a USCG license to carry the maximum number of passengers as per the COI and also the gross tonnage of the vessel along with the navigation route. They carry 7+ passengers.)*

    d. _____ **head boats** *(A head boat is a vessel that has a USCG COI that generally carries a minimum of 50 passengers and charges a fee per passenger, for a specified navigation route. There may be a minimum number of passengers required in order to depart on the trip. The operator must possess a USCG license that specifies at a minimum the number of passengers allowed on the vessel for the gross tonnage and navigation route.)*

*QUESTIONS 2-24 ARE FOR EACH VESSEL OWNED. IF YOU OWN MULTIPLE VESSELS, PLEASE MAKE A COPY OF PAGE 1 AND PAGE 2 BEFORE RECORDING INFORMATION.

2. Is this vessel kept on the water or trailered? ☐ Docked / ☐ Trailered

3. In what city/town is the vessel docked, moored or launched (if trailered) the majority of the time? (City/Town) _____ (State) _____

4. What percentage of your trips in 2010 originated from this location? _____ (%)

5. What percentage of this vessel's trips in 2010 targeted highly migratory species? _____ %

6. What is the overall length of the vessel? _____ (feet)

7. What is the total horsepower of the vessel? _____ (hp)

8. Are the engines a (select one)?: ☐ 4 stroke gas / ☐ 2 stroke gas / ☐ diesel

9. What is the legal passenger capacity of the vessel? _____ (number)

10. What year was this vessel's hull built? _____ (YYYY)

11. What hull material was used in this vessel's hull (choose one)?

☐ Wood / ☐ Fiberglass / ☐ Aluminum / ☐ Steel / ☐ Other

12. What year did you purchase or acquire this vessel? _____ (YYYY)

13. What was the purchase price of the vessel? $ _____

a. Did you purchase this vessel new? ☐ Yes / ☐ No

14. What is the estimated current market value (used) of the vessel if you were to sell it today? $ _____

See http://www.nadaguides.com/Boats to estimate current market value.

15. What is the number of full-time crewmembers during the season (not including the captain) on the vessel? _____ (number of full-time crew)

16. What is the number of part-time crewmembers during the season (not including the captain) on the vessel? _____ (number of part-time crew)

FOR EACH TYPE OF TRIP THAT EACH VESSEL TAKES

17. Do you offer half day fishing trips on this vessel?

☐ Yes (go to Q17a) / ☐ No (skip to Q18)

a. How many Y2 day trips did you take in 2010? _____ (number of trips)

b. Please break out the number of Y2 day trips you took in each of the following periods.

The Economics of the Recreational for-hire Fishing Industry ... 101

January – March	April – June	July – September	October - December

    c. How many Y2 day trips did you donate to charity in 2010? _____ (number of trips)

    d. How long is the typical Y2 day trip? _____ (hours)

    e. On average, how many passengers do you take on Y2 day trips? _____ (number of passengers)

    f. What percentage of your Y2 day trips took place in Federal waters? _____ (%)

If you own multiple vessels, please make a copy of this page before recording any information.

    18. Do you offer full day fishing trips on this vessel?
    ☐ Yes (go to Q18a) / ☐ No (skip to Q19)

    a. If yes, how many full day trips did you take in 2010? _____ (number of trips)

    b. Please break out the number of full day trips you took in each of the following periods.

January – March	April – June	July – September	October - December

    c. How many full day trips did you donate to charity in 2010? _____ (number of trips)

    d. How long is the typical full day trip? _____ (hours)

    e. On average, how many passengers do you take on full day trips? _____ (number of passengers)

    f. What percentage of your full day trips took place in Federal waters? _____ (%)

    19. Do you offer overnight fishing trips on this vessel?
    ☐ Yes (go to Q19a) / ☐ No (skip to Q20)

    a. If yes, how many overnight trips did you take in 2010? _____ (number of trips)

b. Please break out the number of overnight trips you took in each of the following periods.

January – March	April – June	July – September	October - December

    c. How many overnight trips did you donate to charity in 2010? _____ (number of trips)
    d. How long is the typical overnight trip? _____ (hours)
    e. On average, how many passengers do you take on overnight trips? _____ (number of passengers)
    f. What percentage of your overnight trips took place in Federal waters? _____ (%)

20. Do you offer any other fishing trip lengths on this vessel?
    ☐ Yes (go to Q20a) / ☐ No (skip to Q21)

    a. If yes, how long is this type of trip? _____ (hours)
    b. What do you call this type of trip?
    _____

    c. How many of this type of trip did you take in 2010? _____ (number of trips)
    d. Please break out the number of this type of trip you took in each of the following periods.

January – March	April – June	July – September	October - December

    e. How many of this type of trip did you donate to charity in 2010? _____ (number of trips)
    f. On average, how many passengers do you take on this type of trip? _____ (number of passengers)
    g. What percentage of these trips took place in Federal waters? _____ (%)

21. Do you ever take trips without patrons for the purpose of catching bait for your charter operation?
    ☐ Yes (go to Q21a) / ☐ No (skip to Q22)
    a. How many trips did you take in 2010 exclusively to catch bait? _____ (number of trips)

b. Typically how long are your bait trips? _____ (hours)

22. Do you ever take trips without patrons for the purpose of scouting locations and conditions?
   □ Yes (go to Q22a) / □ No (skip to Q23)
   a. How many trips did you take in 2010 exclusively to scout? _____ (number of trips)
   b. Typically how long are your scouting trips? _____ (hours)

23. Do you charter the boat for nonfishing trips like sightseeing, whale watching or bird watching?
   □ Yes (go to Q23a) / □ No (skip to Q24)
   a. How many nonfishing trips do you take in 2010? _____ (number of trips)

24. How much did you earn from fees on a typical trip in 2010?

Fees	Half day	Full day	Overnight
Charter (boat) fees or Head boat (per person) fees	$	$	$

TOTAL ANNUAL REVENUE - QUESTION 25 PERTAINS TO THE BUSINESS AS A WHOLE, INCLUDING ALL VESSELS IF MULTIPLE BOATS ARE OWNED.

25. What was your total annual revenue (gross) from the following items in 2010?

Category	Total Revenue ($)
Income from charter fees	
Income from tips and fish cleaning	
Income from the sale of food and drink	
Income from souvenirs	
Income from the sale of fish	
Income from commercial fishing	

(Continued)

Category	Total Revenue ($)
Income from other charter activities like bird watching trips, whale watching trips, sunset cruises, etc.	
Other income (list)	
TOTAL	

DEBT AND DEBT SERVICE

26. Was there a loan outstanding on any of your vessels during any part of 2010?

☐ Yes (go to Q26a) / ☐ No (skip to Q27)
a. What was the monthly payment (principle and interest) during 2010? $ _____
b. What is the outstanding balance on this loan at the end of 2010? $ _____
c. What was the total amount of your original loan? $ _____
d. What is the term of your current loan? _____ (years)
e. What is interest rate on this loan? _____ (%)
f. Was your home used to secure this loan?
☐ Yes (go to Q26g) / ☐ No (skip to Q27)
g. What percentage of the value was secured with your home? _____ (%)

27. In 2010, did you have any outstanding short term operating loans?
☐ Yes (go to Q27a) / ☐ No (skip to Q28)
a. What was the monthly payment (principle and interest) during 2010? $ _____
b. What is the outstanding balance on this loan at the end of 2010? $ _____
c. What was the total amount of your original loan? $ _____
d. What is the term of your current loan? _____ (years)
e. What is interest rate on this loan? _____ (%)
f. Was (were) your vessel(s) used to secure this loan? ☐ Yes / ☐ No
g. Was your home used to secure this loan? ☐ Yes (go to Q27h) / ☐ No (skip to Q28)

h. What percentage of the value was secured with your home? _____ (%)

28. In 2010, did you have an outstanding loan on a company owned vehicle?
□ Yes (go to Q28a) / □ No (skip to Q29)
a. What was the monthly payment (principle and interest) during 2010?
$ _____

29. In 2010, did you have an outstanding loan on any company owned buildings and/or land?
□ Yes (go to Q29a) / □ No (skip to Q30)
a. What was the monthly payment (principle and interest) during 2010?
$ _____

TOTAL ANNUAL COSTS

30. What were your total annual expenditures on the following items in 2010?

Category	Total Expenditure ($)
a. Fuel and Oil	
b. Captain's share	
c. Crew/mate share	
d. Office staff	
e. Bait	
f. Ice	
g. Food and drink	
h. State fishing permits	
i. Federal permits (HMS/tuna permit, USCG registration, etc.)	
j. Fishing gear and tackle	
k. Other supplies (cleaning, etc.)	
l. Electronics purchased in 2010 (radio, nav, fish finding, etc.)	
m. Engine repair and boat maintenance by boatyard	
n. Engine repair and boat maintenance by your own staff	

(Continued)

Category	Total Expenditure ($)
o. Fishing association dues	
p. Professional certifications	
q. Accounting/book keeping	
r. Bank fees	
s. Legal fees	
t. Advertising and promotion	
u. Booking agent fees	
v. Dock/slip fees	
w. Insurance payments	
x. Telephone (and Internet, if applicable)	
y. Electric and other utilities	
z. Weather service subscriptions	
aa. Company vehicle lease	
bb. Company vehicle maintenance	
cc. Building lease	
dd. Building maintenance	
ee. Lodging related to providing trips	
ff. Meals related to providing trips	
gg. Trailer maintenance	
hh. Tow vehicle gas	
ii. Tow vehicle maintenance	
jj. Tolls	
kk. Boat launching and parking	
ll. Other (specify)	
TOTAL ANNUAL EXPENDITURES IN 2010	

31. Net revenue = (Q25 TOTAL) - ((Q26a×12) + (Q27a×12) + (Q28a×12) + (Q29a×12) + Q30 TOTAL)

Does this value seem accurate? ☐ Yes (go to Q32) / ☐ No (go to Q31a)

a. If no, is it too high or too low? If too high, what expenses have you left out or what revenues have you overestimated? If too low, what revenue have you left out or what costs have you overestimated? Amend above responses if necessary.

32. Is calculated net revenue negative? ☐ Yes (go to Q33) / ☐ No (skip to Q35)

33. Did you operate at a loss in 2010? ☐ Yes (go to Q34) / ☐ No (go back to Q31)

34. Other than in 2010, do you typically earn a profit taking people fishing? ☐ Yes (go to Q34b) / ☐ No (go to Q34a)
   a. Why do you take people out fishing? _____
   b. What changed in 2010? _____

RESPONDENT CHARACTERISTICS

35. Are you an:
☐ Owner/captain OR ☐ Owner/non-captain (go to Q36);
☐ paid captain, private OR ☐ paid captain, corporate (go to Q37).

36. Please indicate your business structure (select one):

☐ sole proprietorship, ☐ partnership, ☐ corporation,
☐ limited liability company ☐ other

37. In what year were you born? _____ (YYYY)
38. How many years have you been a charter owner/captain? ____ (years)
39. What percentage of your personal annual gross income in 2010 was from charter fishing activities? _____ (%)

6.4. Appendix IV: Cash Flow Summary Statistics by Survey Question

Table A19. Charter boat summary statistics by survey question

Survey question	Obs.	Mean	Std. err.	Min.	Max.
Inflow – Gross revenue					
Q25a. Income from charter fees	231	24,547	4,169	200	912,994
Q25b. Income from tips and fish cleaning	207	440	81	0	10,000

Table A19. (Continued)

Survey question	Obs.	Mean	Std. err.	Min.	Max.
Q25c. Income from the sale of food and drink	209	8	6	0	900
Q25d. Income from souvenirs	209	39	25	0	5,000
Q25e. Income from the sale of fish	211	193	107	0	20,000
Q25f. Income from commercial fishing	209	1,997	995	0	200,000
Q25g. Income from other charter activities	214	736	208	0	35,000
Q25h. Other income	205	2	2	0	400
Outflow – Expenditures					
Q26a. Vessel loan principle and interest (monthly)	240	190	24	0	1,800
Q27a. Short term loan principle and interest (monthly)	241	26	8	0	1,250
Q28a. Vehicle loan principle and interest (monthly)	241	17	6	0	684
Q29a. Building/land loan principle and interest (monthly)	241	10	7	0	1,600
Q30a. Fuel and oil	227	4,661	374	100	40,000
Q30b. Captain's share	226	1,169	296	0	40,000
Q30c. Crew/mate share	236	920	183	0	20,000
Q30d. Office staff	236	19	12	0	2,000
Q30e. Bait	233	833	111	0	14,000
Q30f. Ice	233	172	19	0	2,000
Q30g. Food and drink	236	135	24	0	3,000
Q30h. State fishing permits	235	247	20	0	2,000
Q30i. Federal fishing permits	236	69	18	0	4,000
Q30j. Fishing gear and tackle	233	1,336	104	0	10,000
Q30k. Other supplies (cleaning, etc.)	234	483	77	0	10,000
Q30l. Electronics purchased	236	596	91	0	10,000
Q30m. Engine repair and boat maintenance by yard	234	2,001	230	0	25,800

Survey question	Obs.	Mean	Std. err.	Min.	Max.
Q30n. Engine repair and boat maintenance by staff	234	1,002	204	0	38,700
Q30o. Fishing association dues	235	98	12	0	1,800
Q30p. Professional certifications	235	75	11	0	1,200
Q30q. Accounting/book keeping	234	172	19	0	1,800
Q30r. Bank fees	227	51	10	0	1,000
Q30s. Legal fees	234	24	6	0	1,000
Q30t. Advertising and promotion	235	832	77	0	6,000
Q30u. Booking agent fees	235	35	12	0	1,700
Q30v. Dock/slip fees	235	2,097	148	0	9,298
Q30w. Insurance payments	237	1,500	78	0	7,000
Q30x. Telephone (and internet)	233	434	41	0	4,000
Q30y. Electric and other utilities	232	58	12	0	1,200
Q30z. Weather service subscriptions	235	21	5	0	500
Q30aa. Company vehicle lease	237	29	18	0	3,600
Q30bb. Company vehicle maintenance	237	115	31	0	4,500
Q30cc. Building lease	237	59	31	0	6,500
Q30dd. Building maintenance	238	21	14	0	3,000
Q30ee. Lodging related to providing trips	238	39	13	0	1,840
Q30ff. Meals related to providing trips	236	45	10	0	1,000
Q30gg. Trailer maintenance	234	86	17	0	1,953
Q30hh. Tow vehicle gas	232	199	34	0	4,000
Q30ii. Tow vehicle maintenance	234	65	15	0	1,904
Q30jj. Tolls	235	18	4	0	410
Q30kk. Boat launching fees	236	71	18	0	3,000
Q30ll. Other	235	0	0	0	0

Table A20. Head boat summary statistics by survey question

Survey question	Obs.	Mean	Std. err.	Min.	Max.
Inflow – Gross revenue					
Q25a. Income from charter fees	26	202,202	25,752	20,000	500,000

Table A20. (Continued)

Survey question	Obs.	Mean	Std. err.	Min.	Max.
Q25b. Income from tips and fish cleaning	23	942	583	0	11,000
Q25c. Income from the sale of food and drink	24	1,334	644	0	12,500
Q25d. Income from souvenirs	23	109	109	0	2,500
Q25e. Income from the sale of fish	24	0	0	0	0
Q25f. Income from commercial fishing	24	0	0	0	0
Q25g. Income from other charter activities	26	8,892	5,026	0	125,000
Q25h. Other income	23	332	289	0	6,626
Outflow – Expenditures					
Q26a. Vessel loan principle and interest (monthly)	33	806	209	0	4,591
Q27a. Short term loan principle and interest (monthly)	32	198	80	0	1,796
Q28a. Vehicle loan principle and interest (monthly)	33	41	22	0	590
Q29a. Building/land loan principle and interest (monthly)	33	156	114	0	3,500
Q30a. Fuel and oil	22	24,775	3,554	1,200	60,000
Q30b. Captain's share	26	17,014	3,536	0	56,400
Q30c. Crew/mate share	27	18,240	4,074	0	80,000
Q30d. Office staff	26	1,704	753	0	13,500
Q30e. Bait	25	5,498	830	0	14,000
Q30f. Ice	26	195	72	0	1,250
Q30g. Food and drink	27	289	130	0	2,500
Q30h. State fishing permits	26	308	59	0	900
Q30i. Federal fishing permits	29	381	115	0	2,800

Survey question	Obs.	Mean	Std. err.	Min.	Max.
Q30j. Fishing gear and tackle	28	2,827	536	0	10,000
Q30k. Other supplies (cleaning, etc.)	28	1,380	301	0	6,280
Q30l. Electronics purchased	30	1,339	364	0	7,000
Q30m. Engine repair and boat maintenance by yard	25	4,843	1,180	0	26,000
Q30n. Engine repair and boat maintenance by staff	28	4,823	1,065	0	19,500
Q30o. Fishing association dues	27	2596	80	0	1,500
Q30p. Professional certifications	29	112	50	0	1,400
Q30q. Accounting/book keeping	28	1,419	281	0	5,500
Q30r. Bank fees	28	229	71	0	1,200
Q30s. Legal fees	28	257	97	0	2,000
Q30t. Advertising and promotion	24	6,540	1,185	0	16,500
Q30u. Booking agent fees	29	0	0	0	0
Q30v. Dock/slip fees	29	5,430	990	0	18,000
Q30w. Insurance payments	25	6,709	849	0	16,000
Q30x. Telephone (and internet)	26	1,057	221	0	4,000
Q30y. Electric and other utilities	27	456	163	0	3,400
Q30z. Weather service subscriptions	31	0	0	0	0
Q30aa. Company vehicle lease	30	133	133	0	4,000
Q30bb. Company vehicle maintenance	30	138	61	0	1,250
Q30cc. Building lease	31	183	127	0	3,000
Q30dd. Building maintenance	30	67	67	0	2,000
Q30ee. Lodging related to providing trips	31	0	0	0	0

Table A20. (Continued)

Survey question	Obs.	Mean	Std. err.	Min.	Max.
Q30ff. Meals related to providing trips	31	5	5	0	140
Q30gg. Trailer maintenance	31	0	0	0	0
Q30hh. Tow vehicle gas	31	0	0	0	0
Q30ii. Tow vehicle maintenance	31	0	0	0	0
Q30jj. Tolls	29	3	3	0	84
Q30kk. Boat launching fees	30	4	4	0	120
Q30ll. Other	31	0	0	0	0

6.5. Appendix V: IMPLAN Modeling Approach

The IMPLAN system consists of software and data that may be purchased from the Minnesota IMPLAN Group. The software provides the mathematical algorithms to estimate input-output models, as well as a user-friendly interface for customizing input-output models to an application. Default data sets available for purchase include county-level data on the economic characteristics of 440 distinct business sectors for every county in the U.S. County-level data sets for each coastal state in the Northeast, from Maine to North Carolina, were acquired to construct the input-output model.

Unfortunately, the operation of charter fishing boats is included in an all encompassing Scenic and Sightseeing Transportation sector that includes all land, air, and water-related transportation businesses. Therefore, the underlying economic data contained in IMPLAN characterizes the aggregate activity of many businesses and will not accurately portray the operation of charter fishing boats in the Northeast. To more accurately characterize the actual operation of for-hire businesses, total charter and head boat gross revenues, expenses, and net returns, estimated from the survey data (see Table 14), were used in conjunction with IMPLAN multipliers to calculate the regionwide multiplier effects attributed to the for-hire fleet in the Northeast.

Questions concerning products and services purchased from businesses located in the Northeast versus those purchased from businesses located outside the region were not included on the survey. Purchases from businesses located outside of the Northeast impact the economies of other regions and should be excluded from the contribution assessment. Fortunately, the IMPLAN system contains regional purchase coefficients (RPCs), which can be used to estimate the portion of the total regional demand supplied by regional producers. By incorporating IMPLAN's RPCs for all commodity-based transactions, we were able to estimate the amount of each purchase that was supplied by businesses located in the Northeast.[8]

IMPLAN margins were used to convert retail-level prices paid by for-hire owners into appropriate producer values. Margins ensure that correct values are assigned to products (i.e., commodities) as they move from producers, to wholesalers, through transportation sectors, and finally on to retail establishments.

For-hire revenue obtained from both nonresidents and residents of the Northeast were used in the assessment. However, spending by residents of the Northeast on recreation-related activities is part of household consumption and is endogenous in the input-output model. Therefore, to avoid double-counting in the input-output model, the total value of for-hire gross revenue obtained from residents of the Northeast was subtracted from IMPLAN prior to constructing the input-output model. Using this procedure, the contribution of revenue received from resident for-hire passengers can be considered exogenous and was modeled in the same manner as the revenue received from nonresident passengers.[9]

6.5.1. For-Hire Fleet Operating Expenditures

The full list of individual expense items that were applied to the IMPLAN-generated multipliers is shown in Table A21. Several of the expense items warrant further clarification. The cost of supplies was apportioned evenly across four IMPLAN sectors that manufacture soaps, brooms, mops, clothes (e.g., uniforms) and plastic bags. These were the items that for-hire owners most commonly listed as "other supplies" on the survey. A detailed breakdown of food and drink expenditures was not requested on the survey instrument, so this cost was assigned to IMPLAN sectors according to the Personal Consumption Expenditure (PCE) activity data base for grocery store purchases created by the Bureau of Economic Analysis. This PCE vector is available in IMPLAN and represents the national average expenditure pattern by households for groceries. The total cost of state fishing permits, as well as the cost of obtaining professional certificates, was assigned to IMPLAN sectors according to the state/local government noneducation institution spending pattern available in IMPLAN. This spending pattern represents the regionwide average expenditure pattern by state/local government institutions, not involved in education-related activities, and includes goods and services purchased as well as wages and salaries paid to government employees. The total cost of federal fishing permits was assigned to the federal government nondefense institution spending pattern contained in IMPLAN.[10]

Table A21. Charter and head boat IMPLAN sectoring scheme

Expenditure/Income Category	IMPLAN sector(s)	IMPLAN description
Fuel and oil	3115	Refined petroleum products
Bait	3017	Fish (squid, clams, etc.)
Ice	3070	Soft drinks and manufactured ice
Food and drink	PCE, NIPA1111	IMPLAN PCE vector for grocery store purchases
Tackle and supplies		
Fishing gear and tackle	3311	Sporting and athletic goods
Other supplies	3138, 3318, 3086, 3142	Soaps, brooms, mops, knit apparel, plastics
Repair and maintenance		
By boatyard	418	Personal and household goods repair and maintenance
By staff	320	Retail stores - motor vehicle and parts (boat parts)
Insurance	357	Insurance carriers
Overhead		
Office staff	5001	Employee compensation
State fishing permits	State govt	State/local govt noneduction institution spending pattern
Federal fishing permits	Federal govt	Federal govt nondefense institution spending pattern
Fishing association dues	425	Civic, social, professional, and similar organizations
Professional certifications	State govt	State/local govt noneduction institution spending pattern
Accounting / book keeping	368	Accounting, tax preparation, bookkeeping, and payroll
Bank fees	354	Monetary authorities
Legal fees	367	Legal services

Expenditure/Income Category	IMPLAN sector(s)	IMPLAN description
Advertising and promotion	377	Advertising and related services
Booking agent fees	383	Travel arrangement and reservation services
Dock/slip fees	409	Amusement parks, arcades, and gambling industries (marinas)
Telephone and internet	351	Telecommunications
Electric and other utilities	31	Electric power generation, transmission, and distribution
Weather service subscriptions	380	Miscellaneous professional, scientific, and technical services
Company vehicle lease	355	Nondepository credit intermediation and related activities
Company vehicle maintenance	414	Automotive repair and maintenance
Hired captain	5001	Employee compensation
Crew / mates	5001	Employee compensation
Investments		
Electronics	3249	Search, detection, and navigation instruments
Loan payments		
Principal	291	Boat building
Interest	354	Monetary authorities
Owner net returns		
Head boat owners	10008	Households 100-150K
Charter boat owners	10003	Households 15-25K

6.5.2. Disposable Income Spending by Owners, Hired Captains, Crew/Mates, and Office Staff

Calculation of "induced" impacts required making assumptions about the goods and services purchased and the levels of disposable income available for spending. The IMPLAN system contains a PCE activity database that represents the national average expenditure pattern for disposable income according to nine different annual household income classes. Each of the nine household income PCE vectors show the average proportion of goods and services that will be purchased from a given IMPLAN sector for each dollar of spending. Spending patterns differ dramatically between income levels. Low-income spending is more heavily weighted toward necessities (i.e., food, clothing, shelter), while higher-income levels provide more disposable income for recreation and luxury spending. In absence of a primary expenditure survey that identifies the specific spending patterns of for-hire vessel owners, hired captains, crew/mates, and office staff, the nine IMPLAN PCE vectors provide a reasonable approximation of the goods and services that are purchased with the income earned from for-hire activities.

The regional contribution of income expenditures to the Northeast's economy were estimated separately for vessel owners, captains, crew/mates, and office staff, to account for differences in spending across income levels. The average net return, per vessel, for head boat owners in 2010, was approximately $95.2 thousand. Many head boat owners earned additional income from other activities though. Survey data indicated that the average head boat owner derived approximately 70% of his/her total income from for-hire activities in 2010. Therefore, it can be assumed that the average head boat owner earned a total of just over $135 thousand (95/0.7=135.7) in 2010 from all income-generating activities. While the contributions of non for-hire earnings to the Northeast's economy are excluded from this study, the additional income earned by head boat owners had an effect on which PCE profile was chosen to best represent the overall spending pattern of head boat owners. Ultimately, head boat owners were assumed to spend their income according to the spending pattern represented by households with earnings of $100-$150 thousand in 2010.[11]

Charter boat net returns were assumed to have been spent according to the spending pattern represented by households with earnings of $25-$35 thousand. Net earnings per charter vessel averaged $5,175, but charter owners indicated that only 17% of their total income, on average, in 2010 was derived from charter activities. Thus, total earnings from all income-generating activities in 2010 was calculated at approximately $30.8 thousand (5,175/0.168=30,804), and it was assumed that charter owners would spend their disposable income according to the spending pattern represented by households with incomes that range from $25-$35 thousand.[12]

Hired captains, crew/mates, and office staff earnings, were assumed to be spent according to the average spending pattern across all Northeast households contained in IMPLAN (IMPLAN sector 5001, employee compensation). Because of the seasonal nature of the for-hire business in the Northeast, a substantial number of individuals employed by head boat and charter boat owners in the Northeast are likely employed in other industries during the offseason. The survey we conducted was administered to for-hire owners, and not hired employees, so we were unable to determine total annual income levels for hired employees. In the absence of this information, the employee compensation vector provides a reasonable approximation of the goods and services purchased by hired captains, crew/mates, and office staff employed by both head boat and charter boat owners in 2010.

End Notes

[1] Personal communication from the National Marine Fisheries Service, Fisheries Statistics Division July 10, 2012.

[2] A wave specifies a two-month period and the RFHES sampling frame was drawn from the list of vessels considered active during January and February of 2011. The bulk of the survey methods explained here were described in the final contractor's report submitted to the National Marine Fisheries Service, and this report is available upon request.

[3] The training sessions for the screening calls and the telephone and in-person interviews included a description of the goals and objectives of the study, detailed explanations of all questions contained in the questionnaires, an emphasis on the "confidential and proprietary" nature of the data collected, and proper procedures for coding and editing responses.

[4] The operating characteristics of for-hire boats in the Northeast that mainly target offshore HMS (e.g., billfish, swordfish, tunas, sharks, wahoo, dolphin, and amberjack) are fundamentally different from for-hire boats that primarily fish inshore for bottom fish, flatfish, and small game species. Some vessels participate in both inshore and offshore fishing, but most vessels primarily specialize in one or the other. Because of sampling constraints, it was determined that it would not be possible to survey a sufficient number of vessel owners that primarily target HMS so these vessels were excluded from this study.

[5] Although QuanTech conducted call-backs when necessary to fill in missing data or confirm questionable responses from owners who completed the survey by mail/email, they were unable to recontact all individuals so not all missing values and questionable responses were clarified. All surveys completed during in-person interviews and by telephone were complete.

[6] An explanation for this seemingly low estimate of annual net earnings for the average charter vessel is provided below in Section 4.2 Economic Status of the For-Hire Industry.

[7] Vessels in the For-Hire Vessel Directory that mainly fished for highly migratory species in 2010 were excluded, and considerable effort was exerted to remove duplicate vessels that operated in more than one Northeast coastal state.

[8] IMPLAN's default RPC values associated with the supply of bait (frozen fish, squid, sea worms, clams, live eels, etc.) from local fishermen and wholesalers was increased to one, since virtually all locally purchased bait comes from harvesters and dealers operating in the Northeast.

[9] Inclusion of the passenger fees received from both nonresidents and residents is necessary to show the total contribution of the for-hire industry to the Northeast's economy. Failure to include the revenue received from residents would underestimate the contribution of the for-hire fleet. Contribution-type input-output assessments are often confused with economic

impact input-output assessments, where resident expenditures are usually excluded. Further clarification of the differences can be found in Watson et. al. 2007.

[10] Three other expenditure categories were adjusted further prior to generating impacts. A large portion of payments for property insurance and interest on loans generate no economic impacts in an input-output model. The sales of most industries in an input-output model are expressed in terms of business receipts, but the insurance carrier and the banking sectors are measured on a net basis. The output of the insurance carrier sector is calculated by subtracting claims and policy dividends paid from premiums earned. The output of the banking sector includes interest payments on loans, but also many other income-generating activities, and takes into account the interest paid by banks on depositors' funds and for bank services where no explicit charges are made. Therefore, if the total estimated value of the property insurance and interest payments made by for-hire vessel owners were applied to the input-output model's multipliers, the impact on the local economy would be overstated. To provide net expenditure estimates that would equate to the values contained within IMPLAN, the insurance expenditure estimate was adjusted by the average net profit margin percentage for property and casualty insurance firms in the Northeast (7.2%), and the average net profit margin percentage for the banking industry in the Northeast was used to adjust expenditures on bank fees and interest payments (15.3%; http://biz.yahoo.com/p/).

[11] The Household Income Change option was employed in IMPLAN to estimate the multiplier effects of the earnings by head boat owners in 2010. This option correctly removes personal taxes and savings, based on regional average rates, before calculating the contribution of disposable income expenditures to the economy.

[12] Income earned by spouses also contributes to the income base of households and may raise the level of disposable income available for spending. The average level of spousal earnings are unknown, however, so the PCE profile chosen for the analysis is based on personal earnings and not actual household earnings. Additionally, as indicated in Section 4.2, we consider our estimate of average charter net earnings to be a lower bound approximation of earnings. For these reasons, the average household income of charter owners was likely higher than $25-$35 thousand.

In: Recreational Fisheries in the U.S.   ISBN: 978-1-63485-595-2
Editor: Ellen K. Parker   © 2016 Nova Science Publishers, Inc.

Chapter 5

RECREATIONAL FISHERIES MANAGEMENT: THE NATIONAL MARINE FISHERIES SERVICE SHOULD DEVELOP A COMPREHENSIVE STRATEGY TO GUIDE ITS DATA COLLECTION EFFORTS[*]

United States Government Accountability Office

WHY GAO DID THIS STUDY

Almost 11 million anglers made nearly 71 million marine recreational fishing trips in the continental United States in 2013. Pressure on many fish stocks from fishing has increased demand for quality and timely data that can be used to assess the status of various fish stocks as part of managing marine recreational fisheries. The many modes of marine recreational fishing— in which anglers fish from private boats or boats with guides, the shoreline, private property, and public docks— make collecting the data needed to effectively manage recreational fisheries both complex and challenging.

GAO was asked to review NMFS' marine recreational fisheries data collection program. This report examines (1) challenges that have been identified with the agency's data collection efforts for managing marine

---

[*] This is an edited, reformatted and augmented version of a United States Government Accountability Office, Publication No. GAO-16-131, dated December 2015.

recreational fisheries and (2) steps the agency has taken to improve data collection and challenges that remain. GAO reviewed laws, policies, and guidance related to federal and state recreational fisheries data collection methods; reviewed NMFS and other documents on recreational fisheries data collection; and interviewed a nongeneralizable sample of federal and state recreational fisheries officials and other stakeholders, selected to provide geographic representation, among other things, to obtain their views on NMFS' data collection efforts.

WHAT GAO RECOMMENDS

GAO recommends that NMFS develop a comprehensive strategy to guide its data collection efforts. The agency agreed with GAO's recommendation.

WHAT GAO FOUND

The National Marine Fisheries Service (NMFS) within the Department of Commerce faces several challenges related to fisheries data collection, according to reports GAO reviewed and NMFS officials and stakeholders GAO interviewed. These challenges include collecting quality recreational fishing data that are timely for managing marine recreational fisheries and communicating with stakeholders. Regarding the collection of quality data, for example, NMFS faces a challenge identifying the universe of anglers from which to collect information about their marine recreational fishing activity. NMFS relies in part on state registries to identify anglers, but some states exempt certain anglers from registering, and therefore NMFS does not have a complete list of recreational anglers. NMFS officials and other stakeholders have also identified challenges in communicating with stakeholders in collecting recreational fisheries data. For example, several stakeholders told GAO that NMFS has not always communicated with the public about its activities, creating concerns about a lack of transparency regarding NMFS' fisheries management decisions. Reflecting this challenge, in 2014, Louisiana withdrew from the federal fisheries data collection program and implemented its own program because of concerns about federal recreational fisheries data, according to a Louisiana fisheries official.

NMFS has taken several steps aimed at improving data collection to manage marine recreational fisheries and addressing challenges related to communicating with stakeholders. For example, to help improve the quality of the state data it relies on to identify the universe of anglers, NMFS made recommendations to states on improving their recreational angler databases and provided funds to the states to support data quality improvement projects, according to NMFS documents. NMFS has also taken steps to improve communication, including working with Louisiana to perform a side-by-side comparison of federal data with Louisiana's data to determine whether Louisiana's data can be used as an alternative to federal data. However, some challenges persist, including challenges in validating data the NMFS collects and communicating about upcoming NMFS initiatives. More broadly, the agency does not have a comprehensive strategy to guide its efforts to improve recreational fisheries data collection. Such a strategy is consistent with the framework of leading practices in federal strategic planning, as described in the Government Performance and Results Act Modernization Act of 2010, Office of Management and Budget guidance, and practices GAO has identified. Based on GAO's discussions with NMFS officials and review of NMFS documents, the agency has not developed a comprehensive strategy because it has been focused on other priorities such as improving its data collection methods. NMFS officials told GAO that NMFS recognizes the need to enhance its strategic planning but did not provide information about how, or whether, they plan to develop a comprehensive strategy. Without a comprehensive strategy that articulates NMFS' goals to improve data collection and methods for measuring progress toward the goals, NMFS may have difficulty ensuring that the various steps it is taking to improve data collection are prioritized so that the most important steps are undertaken first, and it may find it difficult to determine the extent to which these steps will help it address the challenges it faces.

ABBREVIATIONS

MRIP	Marine Recreational Information Program
NMFS	National Marine Fisheries Service
NOAA	National Oceanic and Atmospheric Administration

United States Government Accountability Office

December 8, 2015

Congressional Requesters

Saltwater recreational fishing in the United States makes significant contributions to local and regional economies and is an important social activity for individuals, families, and communities. Almost 11 million anglers made nearly 71 million marine recreational fishing trips in the continental United States in 2013, according to National Marine Fisheries Service (NMFS) statistics. NMFS, within the Department of Commerce's National Oceanic and Atmospheric Administration (NOAA), acts as a steward of living marine resources through science-based conservation and management. Much of this work occurs under the Magnuson-Stevens Fishery Conservation and Management Act, which sets forth standards for the conservation and management of fisheries resources.[1] NMFS collaborates with stakeholders, such as states and interstate marine fisheries commissions, primarily through its Marine Recreational Information Program (MRIP) to collect and analyze marine recreational fisheries data. Several states, such as Louisiana and Texas, also manage their own marine recreational fisheries data collection programs. In addition, NMFS and its partners collect other types of data, such as information on commercial fishing activity and data on the total size of fish stock populations.[2] The various data that are collected and analyzed are used to estimate fishing activity, understand fish biology, and determine fish stock abundance. This information is used to support the development of annual catch limits and other accountability measures to prevent overfishing and support rebuilding plans for overfished stocks in federal waters.

Pressure on many fish stocks from fishing has increased the demand for high-quality and timely data that can be used to assess the status of various fish stocks as part of managing marine recreational fisheries.

However, in contrast to commercial fisheries, which have standard mechanisms for data collection, the many modes of marine recreational fishing—in which anglers fish from private boats or boats with guides, from the shoreline, from private property, and from public docks—make collecting the data needed to effectively manage recreational fisheries complex and challenging. Designing marine recreational fishing surveys that provide high-quality and timely data at an acceptable cost was identified as one of several challenges facing NMFS by a 2006 National Research Council report on NMFS' marine recreational fisheries data collection methods.[3]

You asked us to examine NMFS' marine recreational fisheries data collection program. This report examines (1) the challenges that have been identified with NMFS' data collection efforts for managing marine recreational fisheries and (2) the steps NMFS has taken to improve data collection and challenges that remain.

To conduct our work, we reviewed and analyzed relevant laws, agency policies, guidance, and other documentation related to fisheries data collection, including specific federal and state marine recreational fisheries data collection projects. To determine the challenges that have been identified with NMFS' data collection efforts, we first reviewed reports and evaluations of NMFS' data collection programs since 2006, including reports from the National Research Council and NMFS, among others. We also interviewed officials from NMFS headquarters and NMFS' Northeast, Northwest, and Southeast regional Fisheries Science Centers; representatives of the Gulf of Mexico, Pacific, and South Atlantic Fishery Management Councils; officials from the Atlantic, Gulf, and Pacific States Marine Fisheries Commissions; and officials from state fisheries agencies in Alabama, Florida, Louisiana, Mississippi, North Carolina, Rhode Island, Texas, and Washington. We selected federal and state agencies and regional organizations to interview based on such factors as geographic representation, locations of large volumes of recreational fishing, and representation from key data collection and management stakeholders. In addition, we interviewed selected marine recreational fisheries stakeholders, such as recreational anglers, to gather information on recreational fisheries data collection methods, associated challenges, and steps taken to address those challenges. These stakeholders represented various geographic locations and different recreational fishing sectors. We determined that the selection of these entities and individuals was appropriate for our design and objectives, and that the selection would generate valid and reliable evidence to support our work. The results of our interviews cannot be generalized to all stakeholders or data collection activities, but they provide examples of different recreational fisheries data collection efforts and challenges. Because the NMFS statistical surveys cover a wide range of methods, apply to a wide diversity of locations, and often entail in-depth technical knowledge about fisheries data collection, we did not conduct a technical evaluation of these challenges or assess their technical validity.

To determine the steps NMFS has taken to improve data collection and challenges that remain, we conducted interviews as described above and reviewed NMFS reports and other documents. Specifically, we reviewed

NMFS' strategic plans, recreational fisheries planning documents, and recreational fisheries data collection program documents. We compared this information with the framework of leading practices in federal strategic planning contained in the Government Performance and Results Act of 1993, the Government Performance and Results Act Modernization Act of 2010, and Office of Management and Budget guidance. We also compared this information to key practices related to communication we identified in previous reports.[4] Consistent with our approach to the previous objective, we did not conduct a technical evaluation of NMFS' steps to improve data collection or assess the appropriateness of those steps in light of the challenges NMFS faces. Appendix I contains a more detailed description of our objectives, scope, and methodology.

We conducted this performance audit from July 2014 to December 2015 in accordance with generally accepted government auditing standards. Those standards require that we plan and perform the audit to obtain sufficient, appropriate evidence to provide a reasonable basis for our findings and conclusions based on our audit objectives. We believe that the evidence obtained provides a reasonable basis for our findings and conclusions based on our audit objectives.

BACKGROUND

NMFS' mission is to act as a steward of the nation's ocean resources and their habitats. This includes responsibility for managing recreational fisheries in federal waters. These waters generally include the United States Exclusive Economic Zone, which typically begins approximately 3 geographical miles from land and extends 200 nautical miles from land. Coastal states generally maintain responsibility for managing fisheries in waters that extend approximately 3 geographical miles from their coastlines. The extent of recreational fishing varies by region, with the greatest amount of marine recreational fishing taking place in the Gulf of Mexico, followed by the South Atlantic and Mid-Atlantic, according to NMFS statistics. Figure 1 shows NMFS statistics about the extent of marine recreational fishing activity overall and the locations of the highest levels of marine recreational fishing activity.

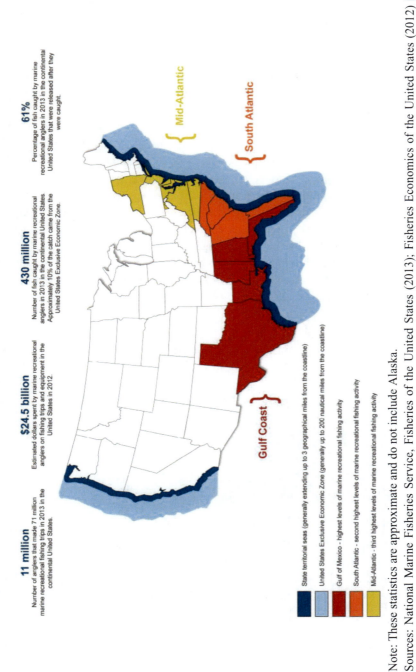

Note: These statistics are approximate and do not include Alaska.
Sources: National Marine Fisheries Service, Fisheries of the United States (2013); Fisheries Economics of the United States (2012) | GAO-16-131.

Figure 1. Marine Recreational Fishing Statistics and Locations of Highest Fishing Activity.

The 1976 Magnuson-Stevens Fishery Conservation and Management Act, as amended, governs marine fisheries management in federal waters, including both commercial and recreational fishing. In the original act of 1976, Congress found that international fishery agreements had not been effective in preventing or terminating overfishing. To manage fisheries and promote conservation, the act created eight Regional Fishery Management Councils, which include representatives from member states and NMFS. The act was amended in 1996 to rebuild overfished fisheries, protect essential fish habitat, and reduce bycatch,[5] among other things. The 1996 act included requirements for NMFS and the councils to develop fisheries management plans for fish stocks and to establish required time frames for rebuilding fish stocks that are overfished. A reauthorization of the act was passed in 2006 and established further legal requirements to guide fisheries data collection and management, including mandates on the use of science-based annual catch limits. Under NMFS guidelines, plans should include accountability measures to prevent catch from exceeding the annual catch limit. These measures can include fishing season closures, closures of specific areas, changes in bag limits, or other appropriate management controls.

Recreational Anglers Use Different Modes to Fish

Private boats and shoreside

Source: U.S. Environmental Protection Agency. | GAO-16-131
Private recreational anglers use private boats and sites on shore, such as public docks or private boat clubs, to access marine recreational fisheries.

For-hire fleet

Source: National Oceanic and Atmospheric Administration. | GAO-16-131.
Private recreational anglers also rely on the for-hire sector, which consists of charter boats and "head boats." Charter boats commonly carry six or fewer passengers who purchase the services of a boat and crew. "Head boats" carry more than six passengers, with each individual angler paying a fee to go fishing.

The marine recreational fishing sector is divided between private anglers and the for-hire sector. Private anglers primarily access marine recreational fisheries by using private boats or by fishing from sites on shore. The for-hire sector includes both charter boats and "head boats." Charter boats are chartered or contracted by anglers for a fishing trip for a flat fee regardless of the number of anglers on the boat.[6] "Head boats" are usually large capacity multipassenger vessels that charge each angler a per person fee for a fishing trip.

Entities Involved in Recreational Fisheries Data Collection

NMFS has overall responsibility for collecting data to manage federal fisheries. It has several offices involved in fisheries data collection and management, including the Office of Science and Technology, six regional Fisheries Science Centers, and five regional offices. NMFS has numerous partners for collecting data to manage recreational fisheries, including coastal states and three interstate marine fisheries commissions.[7] In addition, NMFS and these partners collaborate with regional fisheries information networks, such as the Gulf Fisheries Information Network and the Atlantic Coastal Cooperative Statistics Program, to collect and manage fisheries data.[8] NMFS also collaborates with eight Regional Fishery Management Councils that are responsible for fisheries conservation and management in specific geographic regions of the country. In addition, NMFS collaborates with numerous other stakeholders, such as private anglers, charter boat operators, seafood dealers, nongovernmental organizations, and recreational fisheries associations, to gather input about fisheries data collection programs and management. Figure 2 shows key stakeholders involved in recreational fisheries data collection.

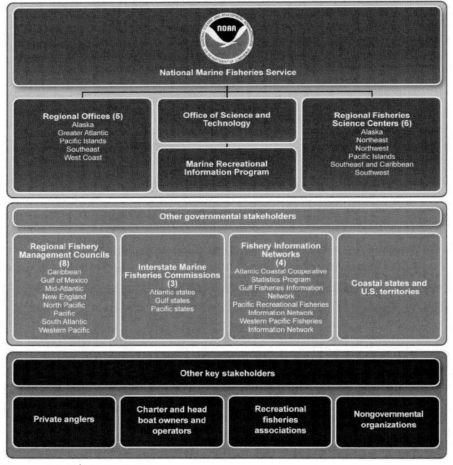

Source: GAO. | GAO-16-131.

Figure 2. Key Stakeholders in Marine Recreational Fisheries Data Collection and Management.

Collection and Use of Recreational Fisheries Data

NMFS and its stakeholders collect several types of data for use in recreational fisheries management. For example, information is collected on recreational fishing effort and catch rates. Effort measures the number of angler trips, while catch rates measure the average number and size of fish, by species, that are brought to shore, caught and used as bait, or discarded (i.e., caught but then released alive or dead). These data are used to estimate the total recreational fishing catch to determine the impact of recreational fishing activity on fish stock mortality and the changes that are occurring to the fish stock over time. Figure 3 shows how these data are used to estimate total catch.[9]

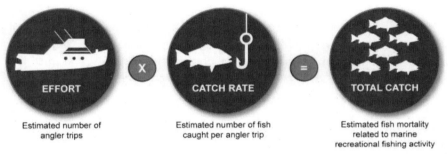

Note: According to NMFS officials, it is likely that some fish that are caught and released alive will survive, but the proportion of caught fish that survive will vary among species, which affects the total catch.
Source: National Marine Fisheries Service. | GAO-16-131.

Figure 3. Estimating Total Marine Recreational Fisheries Catch.

According to NMFS documentation, data on catch and discards are generally collected through shoreside interviews of anglers at public access fishing sites, primarily through NMFS' MRIP Access Point Angler Intercept Survey, which covers the Atlantic and Gulf coasts from Louisiana to Maine, or through state survey programs. These data may also be collected through the use of onboard observers, typically on charter boats or head boats. Data on fishing effort are collected through MRIP or state programs, using methods such as phone or mail surveys, shoreside interviews, onboard observers, logbooks, boat and boat trailer counts, and electronic monitoring or electronic reporting tools. Given the involvement of the interstate fisheries commissions and states in data collection efforts, methods for collecting data on recreational fishing vary among states and regions.

In addition, according to NMFS documentation, biological samples of fish specimens are collected for scientific analysis to provide information on the health and biology of fish stocks. For example, data are collected on the lengths, weights, and ages of fish samples. These samples are often collected during NMFS' shoreside interviews of recreational anglers or by tagging fish to track after they are caught and released. Academic programs and cooperative research with the fishing industry are other sources of biological sampling data.

In addition to collecting data on marine recreational fisheries, NMFS and its stakeholders, such as states, collect other types of data including data on commercial fisheries. Unlike recreational fisheries data, however, commercial fisheries data are collected through a census of the weight and value of all fish species sold to seafood dealers using a network of cooperative agreements with states. According to NMFS documentation, in some regions, state fishery agencies are the primary collectors of commercial fisheries data that they receive from seafood dealers who submit periodic reports on the amount and value of the various fish species they purchase. In addition, independently from recreational or commercial fishing data collection efforts, NMFS and its stakeholders also collect information on the abundance of fish stocks and environmental conditions in fish habitats, such as seafloors, open ocean water, and natural and artificial reefs. These data are used to determine the size, age composition, and distribution of fish stocks, and allow NMFS to track the total abundance of fish stocks over time. NMFS officials told us NMFS relies on its own research vessels or contracted commercial fishing vessels to collect abundance data.

NMFS uses these various types of data to conduct fish stock assessments that estimate, among other things, the population of fish stocks, fish stock productivity, and biological reference points for sustainable fisheries. NMFS and the Regional Fishery Management Councils in turn use the fish stock assessments to examine the effects of fishing activities on the fish stocks and make determinations such as whether stocks are overfished and whether overfishing is occurring.[10] According to NMFS documentation, the data are also used to support management decisions, such as setting limits on how many fish can be caught annually or determining the need to close a recreational fishery for a particular fish stock during an open fishing season, called an in-season closure, when annual catch limits are anticipated to be exceeded.

National Research Council Findings and NMFS' Implementation of MRIP

In 2006, the National Research Council issued a report that reviewed NMFS' marine recreational fisheries data collection programs and made numerous general and specific recommendations to address weaknesses. Among other things, the council recommended the redesign of all marine recreational fishing surveys funded by NMFS.[11] In addition, the council recommended that NMFS improve its survey coverage by either developing a national registration of all saltwater anglers or by using new or existing state saltwater license programs that would provide appropriate contact information for all anglers fishing in all marine waters, both state and federal. The 2007 reauthorization of the Magnuson-Stevens Act included requirements for NMFS to take into consideration and, to the extent feasible, implement the recommendations in the National Research Council report.

Subsequently, in October 2008, NMFS began implementing MRIP, managed in NMFS' Office of Science and Technology, to collect recreational fisheries effort and catch data and develop estimates for use in fisheries management. MRIP was intended to coordinate collaborative efforts among NMFS and its various stakeholders to develop and implement an improved recreational fisheries statistics program. MRIP consists of a system of regional surveys that provide effort and catch statistics for use in the assessment and management of federal recreational fisheries. According to NMFS officials, because counting every recreational angler or observing every fishing trip is not possible, NMFS relies upon statistical sampling to estimate the number of fishing trips recreational anglers take and what they catch. The data gathered from the regional surveys are compiled to provide regional and national estimates. Under MRIP, certain states, including California, Oregon, and Washington, have implemented recreational fisheries data collection programs funded, in part, by NMFS; these data are also used to inform fisheries management. Also, some states have developed and implemented other recreational fisheries data collection programs funded, in part, through mechanisms such as fee-based fishery programs in those states. Figure 4 provides a timeline of key legislative and other events related to marine recreational fisheries data collection and management.

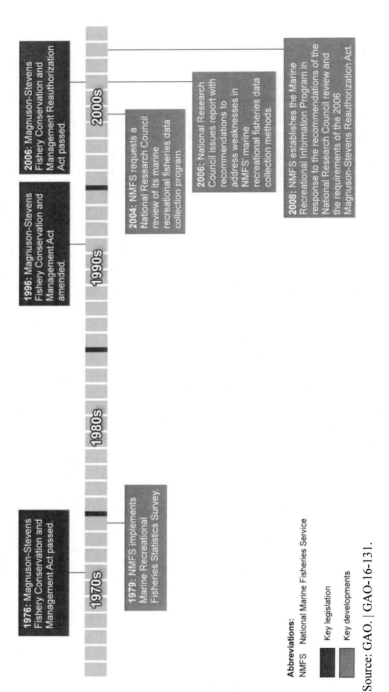

Source: GAO. | GAO-16-131.

Figure 4. Timeline of Key Events in Marine Recreational Fisheries Data Collection and Management.

SEVERAL CHALLENGES WITH NMFS' FISHERIES DATA COLLECTION EFFORTS HAVE BEEN IDENTIFIED

Since the 2006 National Research Council report, NMFS and some state officials have identified several challenges related to collecting data to manage marine recreational fisheries, such as obtaining quality recreational fishing data to inform scientific analyses and produce credible effort and catch estimates. NMFS and some state officials also identified challenges with collecting recreational fisheries data in a timely manner to support certain recreational fisheries management decisions. In addition, NMFS and some state officials, as well as some other stakeholders such as private recreational anglers, identified challenges regarding how NMFS communicates with stakeholders about its marine recreational fisheries data collection efforts.

Examples of NMFS' challenges in obtaining quality recreational fishing data through MRIP to inform scientific analyses and produce credible effort and catch estimates include:

- **Identifying the universe of recreational anglers.** NMFS faces a challenge in obtaining complete information on the universe of recreational anglers. According to NMFS officials, MRIP created a national saltwater angler registry to obtain more complete information about recreational anglers. However, this registry does not include anglers if they are registered in states bordering the Atlantic Ocean and Gulf of Mexico because NMFS granted those states exemptions from the national registry.[12] According to NMFS officials, NMFS relies on state angler registries to identify the universe of recreational anglers in those exempted states. However, some state angler registries offer exemptions from fishing permit requirements, such as for individuals under or over certain ages, and NMFS officials noted that not all anglers comply with state licensing and registration requirements. Therefore, these anglers do not appear on state angler registries. As a result, NMFS does not have a complete list of recreational anglers.
- **Obtaining sufficient coverage in effort surveys.** According to some state officials, NMFS faces challenges in ensuring that it covers the full range of anglers among the participants it selects to participate in fishing effort surveys so that they are representative of the overall angler population. For example, NMFS has relied on its Coastal

Household Telephone Survey, which randomly selects participants from all potential household telephone numbers in coastal counties, to obtain information about shoreside and private boat fishing effort in the Gulf of Mexico and the Atlantic coast. As a result, the survey does not capture recreational anglers from noncoastal states that travel to fish in the Gulf of Mexico or Atlantic coast, or coastal resident anglers in households that do not have a landline phone. NMFS officials acknowledged this limitation with the Coastal Household Telephone Survey.

- **Targeting a representative sample in shoreside surveys.** According to NMFS officials, NMFS faces challenges in collecting data on a portion of the recreational fishing sector since it generally does not collect data on private property or at private-access fishing sites. According to NMFS officials and other governmental stakeholders, this is an issue in states that have many private-access sites, such as California and Florida, because there may be a significant portion of the recreational fishing sector that is not being surveyed. As a result of this limitation, according to NMFS officials and some state officials, NMFS relies on untested assumptions about, for example, catch and discard rates for anglers that use private-access fishing sites to develop recreational catch estimates. However, NMFS officials noted that survey data on fishing effort are collected from anglers regardless of whether they fish from public or private-access fishing sites. In addition, according to one state official, NMFS' standard protocols for determining when and where to assign shoreside observers to conduct interviews may not take into account local fishing patterns and, therefore, observers may not be located in the right places at the right times to collect the most representative data. For example, according to this official, NMFS' protocols for assigning shoreside observers do not account for the length of time anglers would typically take to reach federal waters and return from their trip. As a result, observers may not be at the shoreside when anglers return.

- **Obtaining a sufficient number of survey responses and biological samples.** According to NMFS and some state officials, NMFS faces the challenge of collecting a sufficient number of survey responses and samples in its effort and catch surveys. For example, some NMFS and state officials told us Coastal Household Telephone Survey response rates have been declining, and a 2014 report prepared for NMFS noted that response rates to the survey had "declined considerably" in the previous decade, which could increase the potential for bias in the data collected on recreational angler fishing effort.[13] Also, one state official told us he does not believe NMFS assigns enough shoreside observers to collect the recreational angler catch and discard data needed to develop precise recreational catch estimates. In addition, another state official told us that the lack of shoreside observers has contributed to an insufficient amount of biological samples collected to adequately address scientific needs. Consistent with these views, in 2013 NMFS' Southeast Fisheries Science Center identified a need for more fish tissue samples in its region to aid in assessing fish stock reproduction.

- **Obtaining valid survey responses.** According to some state and NMFS officials, obtaining valid survey responses can be challenging because they depend on anglers' recollections of prior fishing events. NMFS officials told us that the accuracy of self-reported data (i.e., data that rely on participants providing responses based on personal observations) depends on the angler's ability to recall events or to distinguish between different fish species. However, anglers may not be able to accurately recall details about fish they caught and then discarded, especially as time elapses or because of limited knowledge about fish species, and without independent validation or verification, that data may be inaccurate. According to NMFS officials, these challenges affect the Coastal Household Telephone Survey because the survey asks anglers how many saltwater fishing trips were taken in the previous 2 months, but it does not use observers or other mechanisms to independently validate and verify this self-reported data.

- **Obtaining key recreational fisheries data.** According to NMFS and some state officials, NMFS faces a challenge in collecting complete data on discards—that is, fish that are caught but then released—because of the difficulty of validating and verifying self-reported data as previously discussed. In light of this difficulty, Louisiana does not collect recreational angler discard data as part of its own recreational fisheries data collection program because of concerns about the quality of angler self-reported data, according to a state official. Even given the uncertainty in identifying the exact amount of discards, the number of discards can be substantial—for example, according to NMFS statistics, the majority of fish caught by marine recreational fishermen in 2013 were discarded. NMFS officials told us that discarded fish that have to return to great depths often experience high mortality rates due to barotrauma.[14] As a result of limited information about the number of discarded fish and their mortality rates, according to NMFS officials, NMFS relies on assumptions about the mortality rates of discarded fish to produce or adjust recreational catch estimates.

NMFS also faces challenges in collecting timely marine recreational fishing data to support certain fisheries management decisions, according to NMFS and some state officials we interviewed. According to NMFS officials, the Magnuson-Stevens Reauthorization Act of 2006 implemented new requirements that have greatly expanded the pressures on fisheries managers to rely on timely data to make decisions.[15] However, according to NMFS and some state officials, NMFS' data collection systems have not evolved quickly enough to support management decision making. For example, it takes 2 months to conduct the Coastal Household Telephone Survey, which collects data on recreational fishing effort in the Gulf of Mexico and the Atlantic coast, and about 45 days to analyze the data and produce recreational fishing estimates. According to NMFS and some state officials, as a result of these timing issues, NMFS managers do not have enough information to make informed decisions about whether to initiate in-season closures for certain fish stocks with annual catch limits in order to prevent anglers from exceeding those limits. State officials frequently highlighted this as a concern in managing the Gulf of Mexico red snapper, which is susceptible to in-season closures because of concerns about overfishing. According to NMFS documentation, this fishery has been subject to shortened federal fishing seasons over the last few years—including seasons of 9 days in 2014 and 10 days in 2015, compared with 75 days in 2009 and 42 days in 2013.

NMFS, some state officials, and some other stakeholders, such as private recreational anglers, have also identified challenges in how NMFS communicates with stakeholders about its fisheries data collection efforts. For example, a fisheries official from Texas said that, although Texas provides NMFS with marine recreational fisheries data, NMFS does not clearly communicate how or if it uses those data. Some private recreational anglers also told us that NMFS has not always sufficiently communicated with the public about its activities, creating concerns about a lack of transparency regarding NMFS' fisheries management decisions. For example, some private anglers told us they are confused because NMFS has not explained why it continues to shorten the Gulf of Mexico red snapper fishing season even though the red snapper population has increased. NMFS officials acknowledged that NMFS has not always clearly communicated with regional stakeholders to explain its decision-making processes, stating that this has contributed to the public's misperceptions.

As a result of the challenges that have been identified with collecting fisheries data, NMFS officials told us they face a lack of public confidence and trust in their ability to provide the data needed for managing recreational fisheries. For example, according to a Texas fisheries official, Texas withdrew from NMFS' recreational data collection program and implemented its own data collection program in the late 1970s because it did not believe that NMFS' data collection methods suited Texas' needs for managing recreational fisheries. Similarly, in 2014, Louisiana withdrew from MRIP and implemented its own recreational fisheries data collection program, called LA Creel, because of concerns about MRIP data being able to support Louisiana's needs for managing recreational fisheries, according to a Louisiana fisheries official. Similarly, according to state officials, Mississippi and Alabama have also independently initiated efforts to collect data on the abundance of certain fish, including red snapper, in artificial reefs off the coasts of these states because of concerns that NMFS' current data collection methods underestimate the abundance of these fish stocks. Citing dissatisfaction with NMFS' management of the Gulf of Mexico red snapper fishery, the states bordering the Gulf of Mexico released a proposal in March 2015 to transfer the responsibility for managing Gulf of Mexico red snapper from NMFS to these states.[16]

NMFS HAS TAKEN STEPS AIMED AT IMPROVING DATA COLLECTION, BUT SOME CHALLENGES PERSIST AND NMFS DOES NOT HAVE A COMPREHENSIVE STRATEGY TO GUIDE IMPROVEMENT EFFORTS

NMFS has taken several steps aimed at improving data collection to manage marine recreational fisheries and addressing challenges related to communicating with stakeholders. However, some data collection challenges persist, and NMFS does not have a comprehensive strategy to guide its efforts to improve recreational fisheries data collection.

NMFS Has Taken Steps Aimed at Improving Recreational Fisheries Data Collection, but Some Challenges Persist

NMFS has taken steps to address some of the challenges it faces in collecting data for managing marine recreational fisheries, including steps aimed at collecting quality data to support scientific analyses and producing credible effort and catch estimates, improving the timeliness of data collection, and improving communication with stakeholders. However, even with the various steps NMFS has taken, agency officials said that some challenges persist. In April 2015, NMFS requested that the National Research Council review MRIP to determine the extent to which NMFS has addressed the recommendations in the 2006 National Research Council report. A NMFS official told us the National Research Council has initiated the review process, and NMFS expects the review to be completed in 2017.

Addressing Challenges in Collecting Quality Data

NMFS has taken several steps to address the challenges it faces in collecting quality data. To address the challenge of identifying the universe of recreational anglers, NMFS documents indicate that by October 2011 NMFS had entered into memoranda of agreement with states and United States territories that were exempt from the national registry requirements, whereby these states and territories agreed to submit their data on marine recreational fishing participants to NMFS for inclusion into the national registry.[17] In 2011 and 2012, NMFS provided approximately 20 grants to states through the interstate marine fisheries commissions to support initial data quality improvement projects. Subsequently, in 2012 and 2013, NMFS received state angler registry data from each of the exempted Atlantic and Gulf Coast states and entered the data into the national registry database. During this same period, NMFS made recommendations to the states on improving their recreational angler databases. NMFS also continued to provide funds to the states through the commissions to support the initial data quality improvement projects, according to NMFS documents.

To address both regional and national needs for effort and catch data, NMFS has supported the redesign of state and federally managed surveys in all regions. For example, in 2009, NMFS initiated a series of pilot studies to address declining participation rates in telephone recreational fishing effort surveys and potential gaps in the data that could skew survey results due to limitations in reaching coastal residences. NMFS conducted these pilot studies to determine whether mail survey methods for collecting recreational fishing effort data would improve estimates. In a July 2014 report, NMFS stated that the findings from the study indicated that mail survey response rates were nearly three times higher than the telephone survey response rates.[18] Given these results, in May 2015, NMFS issued a plan for transitioning from the current Coastal Household Telephone Survey to a newly designed mail-based survey, referred to as the Fishing Effort Survey. According to NMFS documentation, NMFS expects the Fishing Effort Survey to be fully implemented by January 2018, as shown in figure 5.

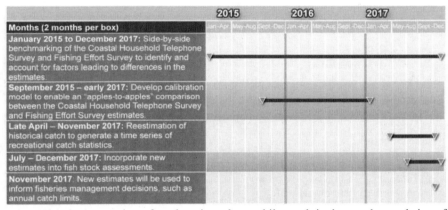

Note: Effort is the number of angler trips taken, while catch is the number and size of fish, by species, that are brought to shore, caught and used as bait, or discarded (i.e., caught but then released alive or dead).
Source: National Marine Fisheries Service. | GAO-16-131.

Figure 5. Timeline of the National Marine Fisheries Service's Planned Transition to Fishing Effort Survey.

In 2013, NMFS also issued new protocols for the Access Point Angler Intercept Survey. Under these new protocols, NMFS assigns shoreside observers to specific locations at precise times to address potential data gaps related to where and when the data are collected. According to NMFS officials, the new peer-reviewed survey design is intended to provide complete coverage of fishing trips ending at public access sites with representative sampling of trips ending at different times of day.

Also in 2013, NMFS initiated a science program review to help provide a systematic peer review of its fisheries data collection programs at its six regional Fisheries Science Centers and Office of Science and Technology. As part of this effort, peer review panels evaluated NMFS' data collection and management programs in 2013, subsequently issuing a report identifying a number of crosscutting national challenges and making several recommendations to address them. For example, the report recommended that NMFS develop a plan for providing the data necessary for conducting fish stock assessments.

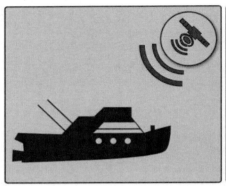 

Electronic monitoring in the for-hire recreational fishing sector includes global positioning system receivers that track vessel locations and pinpoint fishing times to help collect fishing effort data and compliance with fishing restrictions.

Private anglers and for-hire fishing vessels can use electronic logbooks to report effort and catch data, and certain biological data, such as fish length and species.

Note: Effort is the number of angler trips taken, while catch is the number and size of fish, by species, that are brought to shore, caught and used as bait, or discarded (i.e., caught but then released alive or dead).

Source: GAO analysis of National Marine Fisheries Service information. | GAO-16-131.

Figure 6. Examples of Recreational Fisheries Electronic Monitoring and Reporting Technologies.

NMFS has also initiated efforts to evaluate the potential of electronic monitoring and reporting to address quality of data challenges. For example, according to NMFS officials, as of October 2015, NMFS was working with stakeholders in Florida to test the use of a smartphone- and Internet-based electronic reporting tool called iAngler to collect and report data on recreational effort and catch. NMFS is also working with Texas on an electronic reporting tool called iSnapper to test the collection of self-reported catch data, according to NMFS officials. In addition, NMFS issued a policy directive in May 2013 to provide guidance on the adoption of electronic technologies to complement or improve existing fishery data collection programs. In 2013, NMFS began working with its regional Fisheries Science Centers to develop regional plans to identify, evaluate, and prioritize the implementation of electronic monitoring and reporting technologies. According to NMFS documents, each of NMFS' regional offices, in consultation with the Fisheries Science Centers, issued implementation plans in January and February 2015 that include a focus on using electronic technologies to improve the quality of recreational fishing data and data timeliness. Figure 6 shows examples of electronic monitoring and reporting technologies.

However, even with the various steps NMFS has taken, agency officials said that some challenges persist. For example, according to NMFS officials we interviewed, NMFS uses independent checks to either validate self-reported data or estimate a reporting error that can be used to produce unbiased estimates, but the agency faces challenges in independently validating and verifying self-reported angler data. In addition, NMFS officials told us the 2006 National Research Council report contains recommendations that the agency has not yet addressed, including developing methods for improving the accuracy of estimates for the number of discarded fish and addressing the potential bias resulting from the exclusion of private access sites from shoreside surveys. NMFS officials agreed that additional effort should be undertaken through MRIP to evaluate alternative methods for obtaining and verifying discard data. According to NMFS officials, they initiated a process in October 2015 for developing strategies to address these challenges.

Addressing Data Timeliness Challenges

NMFS has begun taking steps to improve the timeliness of its recreational fisheries data to support certain fisheries management decisions but, according to NMFS officials and stakeholders, this data timeliness challenge has not been fully addressed. For example, according to NMFS documentation, in fiscal year 2015, NMFS began studying the feasibility of moving from a 2-month survey period to a 1-month survey period—that is, conducting the survey each month to collect data on the previous month's fishing activity—in its new mail-based Fishing Effort Survey as a way to help reduce recall errors and improve the precision and timeliness of recreational fishing effort estimates. However, some stakeholders told us that NMFS' new mail-based Fishing Effort Survey will still not provide enough timely data to inform in-season closure decisions for federal Gulf of Mexico red snapper seasons.

NMFS officials acknowledged limitations with its approach, noting that in-season closure decisions are based on the previous year's recreational fishing catch estimates. According to NMFS officials, beginning in 2013, NMFS coordinated a series of MRIP workshops with fisheries officials from Alabama, Florida, Louisiana, Mississippi, and Texas to discuss options for improving the timeliness of data to support Gulf of Mexico red snapper in-season closure decisions. NMFS officials told us that they will continue to collaborate with their Gulf state partners to develop supplemental surveys focused on red snapper that can be integrated with the more general MRIP survey approach. According to NMFS officials, NMFS and the Gulf of Mexico Fisheries Information Network recently developed a timeline that describes the process and timing for making key decisions about future red snapper specialized survey methods, as shown in figure 7. NMFS officials told us as of October 2015 the states concurred with the timeline.

According to NMFS and a state official, addressing some of the data collection challenges related to quality and timeliness entails making trade-offs. For example, according to NMFS officials, NMFS also held a workshop in March 2011 with several recreational fishing stakeholders, such as states and councils, to address the need for more timely and precise updates in a short-season fishery. NMFS officials told us the workshop identified several ways in which improvements could be made, but they concluded that more resources beyond what MRIP could afford would be needed to implement those improvements. NMFS' new Fishing Effort Survey collects data on recreational fishing effort that targets many fish stocks, including some that do not need timely data necessary to make fishery management decisions within a shortened federal fishing season. However, according to NMFS officials and a state official, to implement a separate survey that specifically targets Gulf of Mexico red snapper would likely entail adding additional resources to this effort that would need to be taken from other surveys, such as the Fishing Effort Survey. According to NMFS officials, trade-offs also are often necessary to balance the competing needs of state and federal fisheries management and, as a result, NMFS prioritizes among competing demands for data. NMFS has attempted to address the need to understand the trade-offs involved in data collection; according to NMFS documentation, tools intended to help evaluate possible resource allocation trade-offs were expected to be available for use in 2014. However, according to NMFS officials, the tools were not in place as of October 2015, and NMFS has not determined when the tools will be available. The officials said that the tools were being developed in collaboration with academia, but the project stalled because the project leader left the academic institution, and the institution has not yet found a replacement.

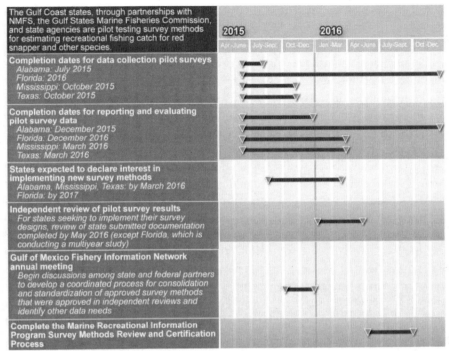

Note: According to NMFS, in addition to the specialized surveys for Gulf of Mexico red snapper, in 2015, Louisiana conducted its own LA Creel survey in tandem with NMFS Access Point Angler Intercept Survey for comparison purposes. In addition, in 2015, NMFS reviewed the LA Creel survey design to determine whether it met NMFS survey date certification standards and will make a certification decision by the end of calendar year 2015, according to NMFS officials.

NMFS = National Marine Fisheries Service.
Source: National Marine Fisheries Service. | GAO-16-131.

Figure 7. Timeline of the National Marine Fisheries Service's Implementation of Red Snapper Specialized Survey Methods.

Addressing Challenges in Communication

NMFS has also taken steps to improve communication with recreational fisheries stakeholders about recreational data collection. NMFS has worked with its MRIP Executive Steering Committee to address priority communication initiatives through various MRIP teams. For example, the MRIP communications and education team plans to implement a communications strategy—entailing various communication activities such as webinars—to support the transition from the Coastal Household Telephone Survey to MRIP's new mail-based Fishing Effort Survey. According to NMFS officials, the agency is developing an MRIP strategic communications plan to guide its transition to the Fishing Effort Survey that was expected to be finalized by the end of October 2015. To further enhance MRIP communications, in 2014, the MRIP communications and education team began restructuring its communications network by developing MRIP communication teams at the regional level.

Some of NMFS' steps to improve communication have resulted in increased collaboration with recreational fisheries stakeholders, according to NMFS and state officials. For example, according to a state fisheries official, NMFS coordinated with the state to provide state officials greater input in determining observer assignment schedules and locations as part of the new protocols for the Access Point Angler Intercept Survey. NMFS officials told us that they are also working collaboratively with Louisiana to perform a side-by-side comparison of MRIP data with data collected under Louisiana's LA Creel data collection program, to determine whether LA Creel can be used as an alternative to MRIP surveys. According to NMFS officials, in early 2016, NMFS and Louisiana plan to evaluate the results of the side-by-side comparison to determine next steps. Regarding stakeholder concerns about NMFS' lack of data on fish stock abundance in reef habitats, NMFS officials told us that NMFS plans to use data collected by academic partners on red snapper abundance on artificial reefs in its Gulf of Mexico red snapper fish stock assessment. NMFS also has worked with the Atlantic States Marine Fisheries Commission and the Atlantic Coastal Cooperative Statistics Program to transition from a NMFS-led data collection system to a state-led data collection approach. In 2016, according to a NMFS official, the Atlantic Coast states will assume responsibility for conducting the Access Point Angler Intercept Survey shoreside interviews to collect marine recreational fishing data from anglers, and NMFS' role will be to review, certify, and provide funds to support these data collection efforts.

NMFS is also placing renewed emphasis on collaborating with its regional partners to determine future data collection needs and priorities for improving recreational fisheries effort and catch surveys, according to NMFS documents. For example, NMFS' 2013-2014 MRIP implementation plan recommended establishing a hybrid approach to MRIP data collection.[19] Under this approach,

NMFS is to maintain a central role in developing and certifying survey methods and establishing national standards and best practices for data collection, while regions—through the regional fishery information networks or their equivalent—are to be responsible for selecting survey methods and managing data collection. According to NMFS officials and NMFS documentation, NMFS staff participated in a workshop in July 2013 to discuss the initial planning stages for developing this new regional approach to recreational fisheries data collection. According to NMFS officials, NMFS is developing MRIP Regional Implementation Plans to address regional data collection needs and priorities.[20] The NMFS officials said that the West Coast region is scheduled to have a Regional Implementation Plan in early 2016. The officials said the Atlantic and Gulf Coast regions support the new approach to data collection and plan to complete their respective MRIP Regional Implementation Plans in 2016. As part of the new hybrid MRIP data collection approach, NMFS is in the process of identifying regional recreational fisheries data collection funding priorities.

Challenges related to how NMFS communicates with stakeholders, however, persist. For example, some Gulf Coast state fisheries officials expressed concerns that NMFS has not provided sufficient information to improve communication regarding its recreational fisheries data collection activities. One state fisheries official said that NMFS has made some progress working with stakeholders to identify MRIP initiatives to improve recreational fisheries data collection, but it has not adequately communicated how it intends to coordinate and collaborate with its stakeholders to implement MRIP initiatives. Some stakeholders continue to express concerns that NMFS is not adequately communicating its process for developing Gulf of Mexico red snapper catch and effort estimates. For example, some stakeholders cited the presence of larger and more numerous red snapper in the Gulf of Mexico and do not understand the need for continued catch limits and fishing restrictions. NMFS officials told us that, although the Gulf red snapper population is rebounding, and the average weight of red snapper that are caught by anglers has increased, NMFS' most recent stock assessment confirms that Gulf red snapper continue to be overfished. Therefore, as required by the Magnuson-Stevens Act, red snapper continue to be managed under a stock rebuilding plan. According to these officials, annual catch limits for red snapper are being reached more quickly due to several factors, including higher catch rates and more fishing effort being directed at the more abundant rebuilding stock. This has required even shorter fishing seasons despite increasing stock abundance, as well as corresponding increases to annual catch limits. NMFS officials stated that, in response to a history of exceedance of annual red snapper catch limits and litigation, NMFS is now setting the length of the red snapper fishing season based on a recommendation by the Gulf of Mexico Fishery Management Council to use a buffer of 20 percent of the annual catch limit.[21] This buffer is intended to account for uncertainty resulting from the difficulty of obtaining timely and precise catch estimates, as well as uncertainty stemming from state regulations that provide for longer seasons in state waters. NMFS officials acknowledged that achieving stakeholder understanding of this complex process is an ongoing concern, but they told us they plan to continue communicating with stakeholders to help convey the rationale behind NMFS' fisheries management decisions.

NMFS Does Not Have a Comprehensive Strategy to Guide Its Data Collection Improvement Efforts

NMFS has taken steps aimed at addressing several data collection challenges, but it does not have a comprehensive strategy to guide its efforts to improve recreational fisheries data collection. The Government Performance and Results Act Modernization Act of 2010 requires, among other things, that federal agencies develop long-term strategic plans that include agency-wide goals and strategies for achieving those goals.[22] Our body of work has shown that these requirements also can serve as leading practices at lower levels within federal agencies, such as at NMFS, to assist with planning for individual programs or initiatives that are particularly challenging.[23] Taken together, the strategic planning elements established under the act and associated Office of Management and Budget guidance, and practices we have identified, provide a framework of leading practices in federal strategic planning and characteristics of good performance measures.[24] These practices include defining a program's or initiative's goals, defining strategies and identifying the resources needed to achieve the goals, and developing time frames and using performance measures to track progress in achieving them and inform management decision making. Furthermore, key practices related to communication call for communicating information early and often and developing a clear and consistent communications strategy to help develop an understanding about the purpose of planned changes, build trust among stakeholders and the public, cultivate strong relationships, and enhance ownership for transition or transformation.[25]

According to a NMFS official, the initial 2008 MRIP implementation plan and the subsequent updates are the key documents used to guide NMFS' recreational fisheries data collection efforts. However, based on our review, NMFS' MRIP implementation plans do not constitute a comprehensive strategy for improving recreational fisheries data collection consistent with the framework previously discussed. For example, the implementation plans do not consistently and clearly define NMFS' goals, identify the resources needed to achieve the goals, or develop time frames or performance measures to track progress in achieving them.

Based on our analysis, NMFS does not have a comprehensive strategy because it has been focused primarily on implementing the recommendations of the 2006 National Research Council report. A NMFS official confirmed that MRIP initially focused on implementing the recommendations in the 2006 National Research Council report and meeting the requirements to improve recreational fisheries data collection as described in the Magnuson-Stevens Reauthorization Act that was passed in 2006. According to NMFS officials, the agency's first priority was to address the recreational fisheries survey design issues identified in the 2006 National Research Council report. Specifically, NMFS determined that it would first design, test, review, certify, and implement new survey designs, such as the new mail-based Fishing Effort Survey. As previously discussed, NMFS intends to transition to a regional data collection approach whereby the agency will collaborate with regional stakeholders, such as states, to identify regional data collection needs. NMFS officials told us that, in hindsight, NMFS could have benefited from a more robust strategic planning approach to MRIP implementation and stated that NMFS recognizes the need to enhance its strategic planning as it begins to transition to a regional data collection approach. NMFS officials told us that NMFS intends to develop strategic planning documents to guide future individual initiatives, using NMFS' experiences with the transition to the new mail-based Fishing Effort Survey as a template, but they did not provide information about how, or whether, they planned to integrate these documents into a comprehensive strategy or how they would communicate such a strategy to NMFS' stakeholders. Without a comprehensive strategy, NMFS may have difficulty ensuring that the variety of steps it is taking to improve data collection are prioritized so that the most important steps are undertaken first and may find it difficult to determine the extent to which these steps will help address challenges. Further, without communicating the strategy and NMFS' progress in implementing it, NMFS may have difficulty building trust among its stakeholders, and these stakeholders may have difficulty tracking the agency's efforts.

CONCLUSION

Recognizing the importance of collecting quality and timely data at an acceptable cost to guide recreational fisheries management and conduct fish stock assessments, NMFS has taken many steps to improve its data collection, such as funding several pilot programs to test alternative data collection methods. NMFS has also initiated a fundamental shift in its data collection approach, envisioning a standard-setting and oversight role for NMFS rather than actual data collection, which is to be carried out by partners. However, NMFS does not have a comprehensive strategy to guide the implementation of its various efforts. Without a comprehensive strategy and associated performance measures to assess progress, NMFS may have difficulty ensuring that the variety of steps it is taking to help address the challenges it faces are prioritized so that the most important steps are undertaken first. Likewise, NMFS may have difficulty determining the extent to which these steps will help address challenges or if a different approach may be needed. Moreover, without clearly communicating the strategy to its stakeholders, NMFS may find it difficult to build trust, potentially limiting its ability to effectively implement MRIP improvement initiatives that rely on data collection partners.

RECOMMENDATION FOR EXECUTIVE ACTION

To improve NMFS' ability to capitalize on its efforts to improve fisheries data collection for managing marine recreational fisheries, we recommend that the Secretary of Commerce direct NOAA's Assistant Administrator for Fisheries to develop a comprehensive strategy to guide NMFS' implementation of its marine recreational fisheries data collection program efforts, including a means to measure progress in implementing this strategy and to communicate information to stakeholders. As part of this strategy, NMFS should clearly identify and communicate programmatic goals, determine the program activities and resources needed to accomplish the goals, and establish time frames and performance measures to track progress in implementing the strategy and accomplishing goals.

AGENCY COMMENTS AND OUR EVALUATION

We provided a draft of this report to the Department of Commerce for comment. In its written comments, NOAA, providing comments on behalf of Commerce, agreed with our recommendation that NMFS develop a comprehensive strategy to guide the implementation of its marine recreational fisheries data collection program efforts. NOAA stated that it agrees that transitioning from a primarily research and development focused program to one that is more focused on implementing improvements to recreational fisheries data collection presents an opportunity to engage in strategic planning. Specifically, NOAA stated it will work with its regional stakeholders over the next year to develop MRIP implementation plans that include milestones, timelines, performance metrics, and resource needs. In addition, NOAA stated that a new National Research Council review of its recreational fisheries data collection program will help to inform its strategic planning effort.

NOAA also provided three general comments. First, NOAA stated that our report disproportionally included interviewees from the Gulf Coast, which may weigh the report's conclusions differently than if other regions were more fully represented. As noted in our scope and methodology appendix (app. I), we selected federal and state agencies and regional organizations to interview based on such factors as geographic representation and locations of large volumes of recreational fishing. According to NMFS statistics, the largest volumes of recreational fishing are in the Gulf of Mexico. As a result, we believe that our selection of agencies and organizations, while not nationally representative, nevertheless provides an appropriate set of perspectives on recreational fisheries management. Second, NOAA stated that it interpreted our statement that we did not conduct a technical evaluation to mean that we are suggesting that a technical evaluation is needed to determine whether NMFS has appropriately prioritized its recreational fisheries data collection challenges. We did not conduct a technical evaluation because it was not within the scope of our review, and it was not our intent to suggest that a technical evaluation is needed. Third, NOAA stated that, while the report identifies several unaddressed recreational fisheries data collection challenges, it does not mention that the challenges require funding levels above the current MRIP budget. Addressing whether NMFS funding levels are sufficient to address the data collection challenges it faces was not within the scope of our review. We do, however, note in our report the importance of making trade-offs in addressing challenges and allocating resources. NOAA also provided technical comments, which we incorporated as appropriate.

Anne-Marie Fennell
Director, Natural Resources and Environment

APPENDIX I: OBJECTIVES, SCOPE, AND METHODOLOGY

Our objectives were to examine (1) the challenges that have been identified with the National Marine Fisheries Service's (NMFS) data collection efforts for managing marine recreational fisheries and (2) the steps NMFS has taken to improve data collection and challenges that remain.

To conduct our work, we reviewed and analyzed relevant laws, agency policies, guidance, and other documentation related to fisheries data collection, including documentation related to specific federal and state marine recreational fisheries data collection projects.[1] We also reviewed previous GAO work related to fisheries management.[2] To determine the challenges that have been identified with NMFS' data collection efforts, we first reviewed reports and evaluations of NMFS' data collection programs issued since 2006 from the National Research Council, the Department of Commerce Inspector General, NMFS, states, and independent consultants and assessed the extent to which they discussed data collection challenges.[3] Of these reports, we relied primarily on the findings of the National Research Council and NMFS to identify data collection challenges. To obtain insights into the challenges identified in these documents, as well as to obtain information on any additional challenges, we interviewed officials from NMFS headquarters and three of NMFS' six regional Fisheries Science Centers (Northeast, Northwest, and Southeast); representatives of three of the eight Regional Fishery Management Councils (Gulf of Mexico, Pacific, and South Atlantic) and all three interstate Marine Fisheries Commissions (Atlantic, Gulf, and Pacific States); and officials from state fisheries agencies in Alabama, Florida, Louisiana, Mississippi, North Carolina, Rhode Island, Texas, and Washington. We selected federal and state agencies and regional organizations to interview based on such factors as geographic representation, locations of large volumes of recreational fishing, and representation from key data collection and management stakeholders.[4] The views of representatives from the agencies and organizations we contacted are not generalizable to other agencies and organizations, but they provided various perspectives on recreational fisheries management. In addition, to obtain additional information about data collected by the recreational fishing sector and challenges associated with data collection, as well as to obtain views on recreational fisheries data collection generally, we interviewed 22 nongovernmental marine recreational fisheries stakeholders. Of these stakeholders, 17 had expressed interest in, or concerns about, NMFS' recreational fisheries data collection to congressional staff. These stakeholders added to the geographic variation and the recreational fishing sectors represented in our review, but their views do not represent the views of NMFS stakeholders generally. To supplement views on recreational fisheries data collection, we interviewed 5 additional stakeholders, including 4 stakeholders identified by NMFS and 1 stakeholder we identified through our previous work on fisheries management.[5] The 22 stakeholders we interviewed included charter boat owners, private recreational anglers, members of academia, and advocacy groups, among others, and represented various geographic locations and different recreational fishing sectors. The NMFS statistical surveys used to collect data for managing recreational fisheries cover a wide range of methods, apply to a wide diversity of locations and often entail in-depth technical knowledge about fisheries data collection. For these reasons, we did not conduct a technical evaluation of these challenges or assess their technical validity.

To determine the steps NMFS has taken to improve data collection and challenges that remain, we conducted interviews as described above and reviewed NMFS' reports and other documents. Specifically, we reviewed NMFS' strategic plans, recreational fisheries planning documents, and recreational fisheries data collection program documents.[6] We compared this information with the framework of leading practices in federal strategic planning contained in the Government Performance and Results Act of 1993, the Government Performance and Results Act Modernization Act of 2010, and Office of Management and Budget guidance. We also compared this information to key practices related to communication we identified in previous reports.[7] Consistent with our approach to the previous objective, we did not conduct a technical evaluation of NMFS' steps to improve data collection or assess the appropriateness of those steps in light of the challenges NMFS faces.

We conducted this performance audit from July 2014 to December 2015 in accordance with generally accepted government auditing standards. Those standards require that we plan and perform the audit to obtain sufficient, appropriate evidence to provide a reasonable basis for our findings and conclusions based on our audit objectives. We believe that the evidence obtained provides a reasonable basis for our findings and conclusions based on our audit objectives.

End Notes

[1] Magnuson-Stevens Fishery Conservation and Management Act, 16 U.S.C. §§ 1851(a)(1)-(10).

[2] A "fish stock" refers to either one species or a complex of comparable species managed as an entity in a geographic area. Throughout this report, the term fish stock is used to mean one fish species or a fish stock complex.

[3] National Research Council, Ocean Studies Board, Committee on the Review of Recreational Fisheries Survey Methods, *Review of Recreational Fisheries Survey Methods* (Washington, D.C.: 2006).

[4] See GAO, *Foreign Aid Reform: Comprehensive Strategy, Interagency Coordination, and Operational Improvements Would Bolster Current Efforts*, GAO-09-192 (Washington, D.C.: Apr. 17, 2009) and *Results-Oriented Cultures: Implementation Steps to Assist Mergers and Organizational Transformations*, GAO-03-669 (Washington, D.C.: July 2, 2003).

[5] According to the act, bycatch means fish that are harvested in a fishery, but are not sold or kept for personal use, and includes economic and regulatory discards. Economic discards are fish that are not kept because the harvester does not want them. Regulatory discards are fish required by regulation to be released after they are caught, or to be kept but not sold. Bycatch does not include fish released alive under a recreational catch and release fishery management program. For the purposes of this report, we refer to bycatch as discards.

[6] In addition to the more common six-passenger charter boats, there are small boats that carry only one or two anglers (sometimes referred to as "guide boats") and very large multipassenger charter boats.

[7] In the 1940s, the federal government authorized by statute three interstate compacts, each creating a regional marine fisheries commission to better utilize and protect fisheries within the consenting states' jurisdiction. The three separate commissions represent the Atlantic, Gulf, and Pacific states, respectively. The commissions were originally authorized only to make fisheries management recommendations to state officials and to recommend coordination among state management efforts. In 1984, the migratory Atlantic striped bass crisis prompted legislation that gave the Atlantic States Marine Fisheries Commission some independent regulatory authority over that species. This authority was broadened in 1993 to encompass other migratory species.

[8] The regional fisheries information networks are state-federal cooperative programs in which NMFS participates as a partner with the state fisheries agencies, interstate marine fisheries commissions, regional fishery management councils, and other federal agencies, such as the U.S. Fish and Wildlife Service. These partnerships engage in cooperative programs to collect, aggregate, and manage state and federal fisheries data to support fishery managers and associated agencies. The regional networks also serve as liaisons for identifying state and regional data needs.

[9] NMFS also calculates the catch per unit of effort to provide an index of the relative abundance of fish stocks over time in certain locations.

[10] We previously reported on NMFS' fish stock assessments; see, for example, GAO, *Fish Stock Assessments: Prioritization and Funding*, GAO-14-794R (Washington, D.C.: Sept. 19, 2014).

[11] This included surveys under NMFS' Marine Recreational Fisheries Statistics Survey, which was established in 1979 to provide data for estimating the impact of recreational fishing.

[12] Section 401(g) of the Magnuson-Stevens Fishery Conservation and Management Act requires NMFS to establish a registry program for recreational fishermen. The law exempts licensed anglers in states that provide data suitable for NMFS' use. Under Memoranda of Understanding with NMFS, each of the Atlantic and Gulf Coast states are providing lists of anglers to NMFS from their saltwater fishing license databases, while Pacific Coast states and island territories are providing survey data to NMFS.

[13] National Marine Fisheries Service, *Development and Testing of Recreational Fishing Effort Surveys: Testing a Mail Survey Design, Final Report*, July 31, 2014. The report did not cite specific response rates.

[14] According to NMFS documentation, barotrauma is a condition experienced by some deepwater fish that are brought quickly to the surface. Fish experiencing barotrauma often sustain serious injuries and, upon release, are unable to swim or dive back to deep water. Therefore, the survival rates of caught and released deepwater fish are generally low.

[15] The act requires NMFS to report annually to Congress and the Regional Fishery Management Councils on the status of fisheries within each council's geographical area of authority and identify those fisheries that are overfished or are approaching a condition of being overfished.

[16] The proposal was signed by officials from Alabama, Florida, Louisiana, Mississippi, and Texas. Two bills (S. 105 and H. R. 3094) pending in Congress would amend the Magnuson-Stevens Fishery Conservation and Management Act to transfer to the Gulf Coast states, under certain conditions, the authority to manage red snapper fisheries in the Gulf of Mexico.

[17] Hawaii, Puerto Rico, and the United States Virgin Islands have not entered into memoranda of agreement.

[18] National Marine Fisheries Service, *Development and Testing of Recreational Fishing Effort Surveys: Testing a Mail Survey Design, Final Report*, July 31, 2014.

[19] An initial MRIP implementation plan was issued in October 2008. Since then, NMFS has issued several MRIP implementation plan status updates that describe various MRIP initiatives and contain information on program accomplishments and priorities.

[20] According to NMFS documentation, MRIP Regional Implementation Plans are to include descriptions of regional needs for recreational fishing statistics, including needs for coverage, precision, and timeliness of survey estimates; a baseline assessment of current data collection programs, including assessing the extent to which current programs satisfy needs and identifying data collection gaps; recommendations and justification for a sequential, prioritized approach for implementing improved methods that address national and regional needs that are currently unmet; and estimated costs overall and for individual survey components.

[21] The council requested that NMFS set the length of the fishing season based on an "annual catch target" that is 80 percent of the overall recreational quota for red snapper. The remaining 20 percent constitutes a buffer to reduce the likelihood of the quota being exceeded.

[22] Government Performance and Results Act Modernization Act of 2010, Pub. L. No. 111-352, § 2, 124 Stat. 3866, 3866-67 (2011).

[23] For example, see GAO-09-192 and GAO, *Pipeline Safety: Management of the Office of Pipeline Safety's Enforcement Program Needs Further Strengthening,* GAO-04-801 (Washington, D.C.: July 23, 2004).

[24] For example, see GAO, *Executive Guide: Effectively Implementing the Government Performance and Results Act,* GAO/GGD-96-118 (Washington, D.C.: June 1, 1996); *Tax Administration: IRS Needs to Further Refine Its Tax Filing Season Performance Measures,* GAO-03-143 (Washington, D.C.: Nov. 22, 2002); *Managing for Results: Enhancing Agency Use of Performance Information for Management Decision Making,* GAO-05-927 (Washington D.C.: Sept. 9, 2005); and Office of Management and Budget, Circular No. A-11, *Preparation, Submission, and Execution of the Budget (*2015).

[25] See GAO-09-192 and GAO-03-669.

End Notes for Appendix I

[1] See, for example, Magnuson-Stevens Fishery Conservation and Management Act.

[2] See, for example, GAO-14-794R.

[3] See, for example, National Research Council, Ocean Studies Board, Committee on the Review of Recreational Fisheries Survey Methods, *Review of Recreational Fisheries Survey Methods* (Washington, D.C.: 2006).

[4] According to NMFS statistics, the largest volumes of recreational fishing are in the Gulf of Mexico, followed by the South Atlantic, and then the mid-Atlantic regions.

[5] GAO-14-794R.

[6] See, for example, National Marine Fisheries Service, *Development and Testing of Recreational Fishing Effort Surveys: Testing a Mail Survey Design, Final Report,* July 31, 2014.

[7] See, for example, GAO-09-192 and GAO-03-669.

INDEX

A

access, vii, 1, 2, 4, 9, 11, 14, 21, 24, 35, 43, 44, 55, 57, 126, 127, 129, 134, 139, 141
accountability, 2, 12, 29, 38, 122, 126
accounting, 14, 80, 90
agencies, 3, 6, 7, 15, 29, 30, 33, 52, 123, 130, 146, 149, 150, 152
Alaska, 55, 56, 125
American Samoa, 58, 59
analytical framework, 76
aquaculture, 3, 36
assessment, 19, 31, 42, 50, 76, 81, 97, 113, 131, 144, 145, 153
assessment techniques, 31
assets, 74, 88, 89
audit, 124, 151
authority(ies), 3, 52, 115, 152, 153
awareness, 4, 13, 15, 35, 37, 46, 47, 51, 54

B

balance sheet, 74, 75, 80
barotrauma, 10, 31, 48, 51, 136, 153
base, 2, 11, 12, 29, 31, 33, 76, 81, 113, 118, 126
benefits, 2, 9, 11, 14, 19, 27, 29, 39, 56, 77, 80, 97
bias, 28, 46, 66, 135, 141
biological samples, 130, 134
boat, vii, 34, 57, 64, 65, 67, 71, 72, 73, 74, 75, 77, 78, 79, 80, 81, 82, 83, 84, 85, 86, 87, 88, 89, 91, 92, 93, 94, 95, 96, 97, 99, 103, 106, 107, 109, 111, 112, 114, 115, 116, 117, 118, 126, 127, 128, 129, 134, 151
businesses, vii, 2, 63, 64, 65, 66, 72, 74, 75, 76, 77, 78, 79, 80, 81, 93, 112, 113

C

Caribbean, 40, 41, 43
cash, 75, 80, 81, 89, 90, 91, 92, 94
cash flow, 75, 80, 81, 89, 90, 91, 92, 94
challenges, vii, 5, 9, 10, 12, 24, 25, 31, 119, 120, 121, 122, 123, 133, 134, 135, 136, 137, 138, 140, 141, 142, 146, 147, 148, 149, 150, 151
charter boat, vii, 34, 39, 64, 65, 67, 71, 72, 73, 74, 75, 77, 78, 79, 80, 82, 88, 95, 99, 117, 127, 128, 129, 151, 152
cleaning, 89, 103, 105, 108, 110, 111
coastal communities, vii, 1, 53
coastal ecosystems, 1, 10, 12
coastal populations, vii, 1
collaboration, 4, 10, 15, 16, 24, 39, 40, 42, 56, 60, 61, 142, 144
commercial, vii, 1, 2, 32, 40, 43, 45, 46, 47, 57, 58, 59, 60, 64, 78, 89, 104, 108, 110, 122, 126, 130

156 Index

communication, 21, 36, 37, 40, 46, 56, 60, 117, 124, 138, 143, 144, 145, 146, 151
community(ies), vii, 1, 5, 7, 9, 10, 11, 13, 14, 16, 20, 21, 23, 24, 25, 26, 27, 28, 29, 30, 31, 33, 35, 36, 37, 38, 41, 47, 53, 59, 60, 95, 122
compensation, 77, 114, 115, 117
compliance, 4, 15, 46, 54
conference, 31, 61
conservation, 2, 3, 4, 5, 9, 11, 12, 13, 14, 15, 19, 25, 29, 38, 41, 52, 59, 122, 126, 128
constituent groups, 41, 47
constituents, 2, 28, 30, 36, 41, 42, 43, 44, 46, 47, 48, 50, 51, 56, 59
consumption, 76, 77, 113
cooperation, 17, 24, 28, 33, 46
coordination, 15, 16, 21, 34, 47, 48, 56, 152
cost, 34, 40, 55, 66, 69, 70, 80, 82, 98, 99, 113, 122, 148

D

data collection, vii, 10, 17, 18, 19, 20, 21, 28, 30, 31, 34, 36, 39, 41, 45, 47, 49, 55, 57, 66, 69, 70, 79, 119, 120, 121, 122, 123, 126, 127, 130, 131, 133, 135, 136, 137, 138, 139, 141, 142, 143, 144, 145, 146, 147, 148, 149, 150, 151, 153
database, 49, 55, 56, 57, 115, 138
decision-making process, 20, 137
Department of Commerce, 120, 122, 149, 150
depth, 30, 66, 123, 151
deviation, 88, 89, 90, 91, 92
disposable income, 115, 116, 118
distribution, 4, 20, 47, 115, 130
diversity, 123, 151

E

earnings, 34, 40, 55, 69, 70, 75, 80, 82, 88, 89, 98, 99, 116, 117, 118
economic activity, vii, 1, 64, 77
economics, 65, 66, 82
ecosystem, 9, 11, 13, 14, 18, 19
education, 13, 15, 60, 114, 144
educational materials, 42, 56
employee compensation, 77, 117
employees, 7, 71, 76, 77, 114, 117
employment, vii, 27, 64, 76, 77, 78, 80, 81, 93
enforcement, 4, 15
England, 32, 33, 36, 46, 95, 96
entanglements, 42
environment, 3, 27
environmental conditions, 130
environmental issues, 16
Environmental Protection Agency, 126
equipment, 42, 81
equity, 7, 74, 80, 88, 89, 94
estuarine areas, vii, 1
evidence, 123, 124, 151
Executive Order, 65
expenditures, 27, 75, 78, 81, 90, 105, 113, 116, 118
expertise, 5, 15, 35, 52, 66

F

FAD, 56, 57
families, 9, 27, 48, 60, 122
federal government, 114, 152
financial, 63, 66, 70, 71, 74, 75, 79, 80, 81, 96, 97
financial condition, 63, 79
financial data, 70, 71, 79, 96
fish, 2, 3, 10, 13, 14, 17, 19, 20, 24, 28, 29, 32, 33, 34, 38, 40, 44, 48, 49, 52, 55, 56, 57, 60, 74, 89, 103, 104, 105, 108, 110, 117, 119, 122, 126, 129, 130, 134, 135, 136, 137, 139, 140, 141, 142, 144, 148, 152, 153

Index

Fish and Wildlife Service, 16, 37, 152
fisheries, vii, 1, 2, 3, 4, 5, 6, 9, 10, 11, 12, 13, 14, 15, 16, 17, 18, 19, 20, 21, 25, 26, 27, 28, 29, 30, 31, 32, 33, 34, 35, 36, 37, 38, 39, 40, 41, 42, 43, 44, 48, 49, 50, 51, 52, 53, 54, 56, 57, 59, 60, 61, 65, 95, 97, 119, 120, 121, 122, 123, 124, 126, 127, 129, 130, 131, 133, 135, 136, 137, 138, 139, 141, 142, 143, 144, 145, 146, 147, 148, 149, 150, 151, 152, 153
Fisherman, 41, 49
fishing, vii, 1, 2, 4, 5, 9, 10, 11, 12, 13, 14, 15, 16, 17, 18, 19, 21, 23, 24, 25, 26, 27, 28, 29, 30, 31, 33, 34, 35, 36, 37, 38, 39, 40, 41, 42, 43, 44, 46, 47, 48, 49, 50, 51, 53, 54, 55, 56, 57, 58, 59, 60, 61, 63, 64, 65, 68, 73, 78, 79, 80, 81, 82, 86, 89, 90, 93, 94, 96, 98, 99, 101, 102, 104, 105, 107, 108, 110, 111, 112, 113, 114, 117, 119, 120, 122, 123, 124, 126, 127, 129, 130, 131, 133, 134, 135, 136, 138, 139,
flexibility, 18, 39
food, 64, 75, 78, 81, 89, 104, 108, 110, 113, 116
food services, 64, 78
for-hire businesses, vii, 64, 65, 66, 74, 76, 77, 80, 112
for-hire head boat, vii, 64, 65
freshwater, 17, 54
funding, 13, 17, 28, 37, 47, 52, 145, 148, 149
funds, 55, 118, 121, 138, 144

G

gambling, 94, 115
GAO, 119, 120, 121, 125, 126, 127, 128, 129, 132, 139, 140, 143, 150, 152, 153, 154
goods and services, 76, 114, 115, 117
guidance, vii, 2, 6, 14, 25, 33, 42, 120, 121, 123, 124, 140, 146, 150, 151
guidelines, 13, 18, 126

guiding principles, vii, 2, 10, 11, 12
Gulf Coast, 38, 39, 138, 145, 149, 153
Gulf of Mexico, 19, 28, 30, 38, 39, 40, 41, 42, 46, 80, 83, 123, 124, 133, 134, 136, 137, 141, 142, 143, 144, 145, 149, 150, 153, 154

H

habitat(s), 2, 3, 11, 12, 13, 14, 16, 17, 19, 20, 27, 32, 33, 37, 55, 59, 124, 126, 130, 144
Hawaii, 57, 58, 59, 60, 153
health, 14, 19, 27, 43, 45, 95, 96, 97, 130
history, 26, 146
host, 21, 28, 53
household income, 116, 118
human, 31, 40, 52

I

identification, 16, 36, 46
impact assessment, 59
improvements, 24, 30, 45, 57, 142, 149
income, vii, 64, 70, 72, 76, 77, 78, 79, 80, 81, 86, 89, 93, 104, 107, 108, 110, 115, 116, 117, 118
individuals, 44, 64, 77, 78, 81, 82, 117, 122, 123, 133
industry(ies), 2, 25, 39, 42, 63, 64, 65, 75, 76, 77, 78, 81, 82, 83, 93, 94, 95, 96, 97, 115, 117, 118, 130
institutions, 61, 114
integration, 6, 34
investment, 74, 75
issues, 6, 10, 15, 16, 18, 20, 24, 25, 26, 27, 29, 30, 33, 36, 37, 41, 48, 50, 51, 53, 54, 56, 58, 60, 61, 78, 136, 147

L

landings, 28, 33, 44, 45, 46
laws, 120, 123, 150

158   Index

leadership, 1, 7, 25, 31, 35, 37, 41, 48, 54
loans, 74, 88, 89, 94, 104, 118
Louisiana, 83, 120, 121, 122, 123, 129, 135, 137, 142, 144, 150, 153

M

majority, 73, 100, 135
management, 2, 3, 4, 5, 6, 11, 12, 14, 15, 16, 17, 18, 20, 24, 25, 26, 29, 30, 32, 33, 34, 35, 36, 37, 38, 41, 42, 43, 44, 45, 49, 50, 51, 52, 56, 58, 65, 66, 120, 122, 123, 126, 127, 129, 130, 131, 133, 136, 137, 140, 141, 142, 146, 148, 149, 150, 152
manufacturing, 64, 78
marine fish, 3, 6, 37, 122, 126, 127, 138, 152
marine recreational fisheries, vii, 34, 59, 119, 120, 121, 122, 123, 126, 127, 130, 131, 133, 136, 137, 138, 148, 149, 150
Maryland, 33, 82, 83
materials, 16, 36, 37, 42, 44, 47, 54, 56, 60
media, 21, 41, 50, 97
median, 64, 71, 79, 80
methodology, 38, 67, 124, 149
Mexico, 19, 28, 30, 38, 39, 40, 41, 42, 46, 81, 83, 123, 124, 133, 134, 136, 137, 142, 143, 144, 145, 149, 150, 153, 154
models, 49, 66, 112
mortality, 17, 18, 28, 29, 34, 35, 42, 48, 56, 129, 136
mortality rate, 18, 136
multiplier effect, 64, 76, 77, 78, 81, 112, 118

N

National Environmental Policy Act (NEPA), 54, 65

National Marine Fisheries Service's (NMFS), vii, 1, 2, 3, 4, 5, 6, 7, 43, 46, 47, 48, 50, 52, 55, 56, 59, 63, 64, 65, 66, 67, 95, 96, 97, 119, 120, 121, 122, 123, 124, 126, 127, 129, 130, 131, 133, 134, 135, 136, 137, 138, 139, 140, 141, 142, 143, 144, 145, 146, 147, 148, 149, 150, 151, 152, 153, 154
National Oceanic and Atmospheric Administration (NOAA), vii, 1, 6, 9, 10, 11, 12, 13, 14, 15, 16, 17, 18, 19, 20, 21, 23, 24, 25, 26, 27, 28, 29, 30, 31, 33, 35, 36, 37, 38, 41, 42, 43, 45, 47, 52, 53, 54, 56, 57, 59, 60, 61, 63, 83, 95, 98, 121, 122, 127, 148, 149
National Research Council, 18, 122, 123, 131, 133, 138, 141, 147, 149, 150, 152, 154
natural resource management, 3, 18
New England, 32, 33, 36, 46, 95, 96
next generation, 5, 9, 31

O

Office of Management and Budget, 121, 124, 146, 151, 154
officials, 120, 121, 123, 129, 130, 131, 133, 134, 135, 136, 137, 138, 139, 140, 141, 142, 143, 144, 145, 147, 150, 152, 153
oil, 30, 75, 89, 90, 91, 92, 108, 110, 114
oil spill, 30
operations, 41, 65, 66, 67, 71, 73, 78, 80, 81, 82, 86, 96
opportunities, vii, 1, 4, 10, 11, 13, 14, 15, 16, 20, 21, 29, 30, 31, 38, 41, 44, 47, 48, 50, 51, 53, 56
outreach, 16, 21, 34, 36, 37, 46, 47, 54, 56, 57, 58, 60, 61, 66, 83

Index

P

Pacific, 28, 49, 50, 52, 53, 56, 58, 59, 60, 123, 150, 152, 153
participants, 12, 15, 26, 27, 29, 82, 133, 135, 138
permit, 38, 83, 96, 105, 133
policy, vii, 2, 3, 6, 7, 10, 11, 12, 21, 25, 27, 31, 96, 97, 118, 140
population, 70, 130, 133, 137, 145
principles, vii, 2, 3, 6, 10, 11, 12
project, 17, 33, 39, 40, 45, 47, 52, 55, 142
Puerto Rico, 28, 39, 40, 43, 45, 153

Q

quality improvement, 121, 138
questionnaire, 68, 69, 95

R

radio, 50, 105
real estate, 64, 78
recall, 135, 141
recognition, 14, 55
recommendations, iv, 29, 41, 44, 46, 57, 121, 131, 138, 140, 141, 147, 152, 153
recovery, 19, 53, 55
recreation, 58, 78, 82, 113, 116
recreational, vii, 1, 2, 3, 4, 5, 6, 9, 10, 11, 12, 13, 14, 15, 16, 17, 18, 19, 20, 21, 23, 24, 25, 26, 27, 28, 29, 30, 31, 32, 33, 34, 35, 36, 37, 38, 39, 40, 41, 42, 43, 44, 45, 46, 47, 48, 49, 50, 51, 52, 53, 54, 55, 56, 57, 58, 59, 60, 61, 63, 64, 65, 66, 79, 80, 83, 96, 97, 119, 120, 121, 122, 123, 124, 126, 127, 129, 130, 131, 133, 134, 135, 136, 137, 138, 140, 141, 142, 143, 144, 145, 146, 147, 148, 149, 150, 151, 152, 153, 154
registries, 120, 133
Registry, 57, 60
regulations, 4, 14, 15, 21, 33, 59, 96, 97, 146
regulatory changes, 35, 36
repair, 64, 75, 78, 106, 109, 111, 114, 115
requirements, 57, 98, 126, 131, 133, 136, 138, 146, 147
researchers, 29, 42, 61
resource allocation, 142
resource management, 3, 18
resources, vii, 1, 2, 4, 10, 11, 12, 13, 15, 19, 20, 21, 23, 24, 26, 31, 33, 39, 44, 52, 58, 59, 66, 122, 124, 142, 146, 147, 148, 150
response, 27, 46, 70, 71, 134, 139, 146, 153
restoration, 3, 13, 14, 55
restrictions, 145
restructuring, 144
retail, 64, 78, 94, 113
revenue, 64, 75, 76, 81, 89, 90, 91, 92, 94, 96, 103, 106, 107, 110, 113, 118

S

salmon, 29, 32, 50, 52, 53, 54, 55
saltwater, vii, 2, 3, 5, 6, 9, 10, 11, 19, 27, 35, 50, 55, 131, 133, 135, 153
Saltwater Recreational Fisheries, v, 1, 2, 6, 9, 10, 11, 12
Samoa, 58, 59
sanctuaries, 15
science, 1, 2, 4, 5, 6, 11, 12, 13, 16, 17, 18, 19, 20, 27, 29, 31, 37, 41, 43, 53, 59, 122, 126, 139
scope, 40, 124, 149
seafood, 128, 130
services, 15, 37, 64, 76, 77, 78, 94, 113, 114, 115, 116, 117, 118, 127
shoreline, 119, 122
shrimp, 83
simple random sampling, 67

species, 12, 13, 16, 17, 19, 32, 33, 34, 44, 45, 46, 51, 56, 59, 60, 98, 100, 117, 129, 130, 135, 139, 140, 152
spending, 76, 113, 114, 115, 116, 118
St. Petersburg, 42, 43
stakeholders, 20, 27, 32, 45, 46, 50, 54, 58, 120, 121, 122, 123, 128, 129, 130, 131, 133, 134, 136, 137, 138, 140, 141, 142, 143, 144, 145, 146, 147, 148, 149, 150
state, 3, 4, 6, 11, 13, 15, 19, 21, 29, 36, 38, 39, 45, 52, 53, 55, 59, 65, 67, 68, 71, 76, 81, 82, 83, 90, 96, 112, 113, 117, 120, 121, 122, 123, 124, 126, 127, 129, 130, 131, 133, 134, 135, 136, 137, 138, 142, 144, 145, 147, 149, 150, 152, 153
statistics, 45, 60, 107, 109, 122, 124, 125, 131, 135, 149, 153, 154
stock, 3, 5, 17, 18, 19, 25, 28, 31, 34, 42, 43, 45, 122, 129, 130, 135, 140, 144, 145, 148, 152, 153
strategic planning, 121, 124, 146, 147, 149, 151
structure, vii, 39, 63, 64, 66, 86, 107
subtraction, 88, 89, 91, 92
survey design, 39, 83, 97, 139, 143, 147
survival, 5, 13, 14, 28, 29, 56, 153
sustainability, 2, 12, 27

T

target, 13, 17, 38, 44, 54, 81, 98, 117, 153
techniques, 13, 16, 17, 27, 31, 33, 42
technology(ies), 3, 5, 16, 31, 41, 141
threats, 13, 58

time frame, 126, 146, 147, 148
trade, 64, 78, 93, 142, 149
trade-off, 142, 150
training, 21, 117
transactions, 64, 113
transparency, 120, 136
transportation, 112, 113

U

United States (USA), v, 7, 41, 44, 63, 64, 119, 122, 124, 125, 138, 153
universe, 58, 76, 120, 121, 133, 138
updating, 46, 47, 48, 54

V

validation, 17, 135
valuation, 19, 34, 35, 50
vector, 113, 114, 117
vessels, 33, 44, 49, 57, 63, 64, 66, 67, 68, 69, 70, 71, 72, 73, 74, 76, 78, 80, 83, 101, 104, 117, 127, 130

W

wages, 76, 77, 114
Washington, 28, 53, 123, 131, 150, 152, 153, 154
water, 5, 25, 29, 30, 38, 100, 112, 130, 153
web, 28, 35, 45, 55, 59
web pages, 28, 35
wholesale, 64, 78, 93